Yum
& YUMMER

Yum & YUMMER

Ridiculously tasty recipes that'll blow your mind, but not your diet!

GRETA PODLESKI

One Spoon
Media

Library and Archives Canada Cataloguing in Publication

Podleski, Greta, author
    Yum & yummer : ridiculously tasty recipes that'll blow your mind, but not your diet! / Greta Podleski.

Includes index.
ISBN 978-1-77504-700-1 (softcover)

    1. Cooking. 2. Nutrition. 3. Diet therapy. 4. Cookbooks.
I. Title. II. Title: Yum and yummer.

RM219.P625 2017   641.5'63   C2017-904997-6

Printed in Canada by Transcontinental Printing PR2

Edited by Fina Scroppo
www.thehealthyitalian.com

Book Design and Video Production by REES + STAGER Inc.
www.reesstager.com

Food Photography and Styling by Greta Podleski
yumyummer.com | greta@yumyummer.com

Author photos (front cover, back flap, pages II, VI, IX, XI, XII, 40, 98, 126, 148, 178, 202, 228, 256, 284, 286, 288, 299, 300, 302, 304) by Hilary Gauld-Camilleri
hilarygauld.com

Published by One Spoon Media Inc. in association with
Granet Publishing Inc.
1241 Weber Street East, Unit 2
Kitchener, Ontario N2A 1C2

(800) 470-0738 | granetpublishing@uniserve.com

If you're interested in bulk purchases of **Yum & Yummer** for your employees or other premium uses, please call us at (800) 470-0738. We offer a very aggressive discount schedule for bulk orders and would be happy to answer any questions you may have.

Recipe analysis calculated using NutriBase Professional Nutrition Manager software (CyberSoft, Inc.). When a choice of ingredients is listed, analysis is calculated using the first ingredient. Optional ingredients are not included in the analysis.

Note: For those with food allergies, intolerances or special dietary needs, always check the labels of food products that you suspect might not be suitable for you. Products like vegetable or chicken broth, soy sauce, barbecue sauce, taco seasoning and oats (to name a few) may or may not be gluten-free. Similarly, marinara sauce or protein powder may not be vegan or dairy-free (they could contain Parmesan cheese or whey protein, respectively).

Dedication

Dreamers

Believers

DOERS

PARTNERS IN CRIME

"The Looney Spoons"

A million memories

A THOUSAND STORIES

INSEPARABLE

It is a blessing to call you
MY SISTER.

Me

Janet

Yes, we have the
same parents!

Introduction

This book is a labor of love. I love food, I love cooking, I love creating something from nothing. In fact, I squeezed every drop of creativity from my tiny brain and injected it into *Yum & Yummer*. Perhaps the image of a squeezed brain isn't the most appetizing or normal way to introduce a cookbook to readers, but I've never really been into normal.

From a young age, I was always curious, adventurous and daring. (Meaning I spent lots of time at the principal's office.) When my friends all got skateboards, I got one too and tried riding it on the school roof. Instead of playing tag or dodgeball or putting Barbie's hair in an updo (or whatever typical activities were popular in my youth), my sister Janet and I built Evel Knievel-style bike ramps that we soared from in death-defying jumps while riding our banana-seat bikes. So cool.

Curiosity about food and cooking set in around age 7, when I marveled at how my mother, despite being a caregiver to six daughters and working full-time, somehow managed to cook dinner every single night. We ate well and we rarely, if ever, ate at restaurants. It seems odd for a child to notice or even care about something like this when, let's face it, my world basically revolved around Etch A Sketch, *The Brady Bunch* and getting into trouble, but I did notice.

I decided she needed help, so I offered to stir, chop, whisk…whatever Mom wanted. It didn't take long for me to realize that cooking was kinda fun, somewhat creative, a little messy (which I loved, especially since my mom always cleaned up) and definitely rewarding. You get to *eat* what you make! Couldn't say that about the sorry-looking macramé plant hanger I crafted in art class (which strangely came back in style). For me, cooking was far more exciting than playing mindless games like hide-and-seek or Kerplunk. I began cooking meals for my entire family, using recipes I clipped from *Seventeen* magazine, even though I was only 12.

At 16, I scored the best job ever (meaning it paid really well!), working in the kitchen at my local hospital, helping prepare meals for patients on special diets, particularly those with diabetes. I worked hard for four years after school, on weekends and full-time in the summer. I loved my job and learned a ton. In my twenties, I applied some of my healthy cooking knowledge and began revamping my friends' high-calorie, gut-busting, artery-clogging recipes "just for fun." My goal was to "healthify" them, whatever that meant at the time.

It was fate that turned my lifelong cooking hobby into a successful business and to tell that story, I'd need an entire book! (If you're really curious and don't already know the *Looneyspoons* story, you'll find "A Tale of Two Sisters" at www.janetandgreta.com.) After writing four healthy cookbooks with my sister Janet (all #1 national bestsellers—am I allowed to toot my own horn? Toot! Toot!), creating food products sold at Costco and co-starring in 39 episodes of *Eat, Shrink & Be Merry!* on Food Network Canada, I've learned a whole lot about healthy cooking and people's attitudes toward it.

First of all, no one agrees what the term "healthy eating" actually means. Why? Because it means different things to different people. There isn't one healthy diet for all seven billion of us. My healthy eating might not be your healthy eating. I might follow a gluten-free diet (I don't) and you might be a vegan, and we'd both believe our way of eating is healthy. Healthy can mean gluten-free, vegan, vegetarian, dairy-free, low-calorie, low-carb, high-fat, no fat, Paleo or whatever, depending on who you ask. And who are we to judge that someone's diet (meaning "what they choose to eat") is wrong? Sometimes I wish I could wave a magic wand over the universe and make everyone less judgmental about what others are eating. You are not right. They are not wrong. Period. End of story. Exclamation mark! (Rant over, thanks for reading!)

And, let's not forget, for many people (I'd argue MOST people), healthy eating simply means using natural, fresh ingredients to make tasty, home-cooked meals versus eating out of packages, boxes and bags and in fast-food restaurants. That's the definition of healthy eating that resonates most with me. I feel best when I eat lots of delicious, home-cooked vegetarian meals and the occasional chicken or fish entrée, with meat (like beef or pork) appearing on my plate about once a month. That's the Greta Podleski "diet" and it works for me. That doesn't mean it's right for you.

Incidentally, I was 20 pounds heavier 25 years ago and I didn't diet to lose the weight, so I must be doing something right! I have more energy now than I did in my twenties. I don't count calories or fat grams or obsess about any numbers at all. I eat when I'm hungry and I don't snack at night. Luckily, I don't have a sweet tooth, but I do love salty, crunchy things (CHIPS!). I mention this because people always ask me, "How do you stay so slim when you're always cooking?" My answer is "I'm slim *because* I'm always cooking!" I have no scientific evidence to back up this claim, but I believe it's true. I control what I eat, I love what I eat (mostly my own recipes—ha-ha!) and I don't stress or fret about what I eat.

I decided years ago that I'd rather not tell people how or exactly what to eat. There's just too much conflicting nutrition information out there and the sad reality is that "experts" can find studies to "prove" every side of every dietary argument. It's frustrating and annoying, actually. Who are we supposed to believe? No wonder people are so confused. I know I am.

My passion isn't preaching about healthy eating, it's helping busy North Americans answer the question "What's for dinner?" It's creating outrageously delicious recipes using common, everyday ingredients found at your local grocery store. Recipes anyone can make. Ridiculously tasty recipes, recipes your whole family will love, recipes you'll make over and over again, recipes that you'll share with friends, recipes you'll talk about at work, recipes that taste so good you'd swear they're bad for you! When you happily spring out of bed every morning like I do, even though you've been working at the same job for 20 years, you know you've found your passion. Either that or you really have to go to the bathroom.

A Facebook fan once referred to me as "the mad scientist of healthy cooking" and I swear it's one of the best compliments I've ever received in my life (besides the time my fifth-grade boyfriend said my Dorothy Hamill haircut was "totally decent"). I'm not sure about the science part, since I'm a self-taught cook (not a trained chef), but creating and sharing healthy recipes is what I love to do and it's what led to *Yum & Yummer*.

I've been writing this book for five years in my head and one-and-a-half years in my kitchen. My dream was to create a truly unique cookbook, a book as innovative and imaginative as my first cookbook, *Looneyspoons*, was back in 1996. My vision was simple on paper yet difficult to execute: Insanely delicious recipes + stunning food photography + awesome how-to videos for every single recipe. No, not half the recipes. All of them. I wanted the videos to inspire people to cook, to help them choose what to make for dinner and to get newbies and kids cooking. And I wanted the videos to jump right off the page and onto your smartphone. I also decided to study food photography so I could take all the photos myself. At times I bit off more than I could chew but I think the end product is pretty darn tasty! I love this book and I'm so proud of it. I pray you love it, too, and that you can feel and see the effort and passion that went into it.

Besides the exciting video element (barcode at the bottom of each recipe), you'll notice helpful GF (gluten-free), DF (dairy-free) and V (vegan) icons on the recipe pages. Your numerous requests for more gluten-free and plant-based recipes have been fulfilled! Hooray! In fact, more than 60 percent of *Yum & Yummer's* recipes are vegetarian, so lettuce eat more plants! There's clearly a worldwide trend toward consuming more meatless meals and I'm on the bandwagon, big time.

For Weight Watchers members who need the sugar content to calculate points, I heard your pleas and I'm pleased to say that every *Yum & Yummer* recipe contains a complete nutritional analysis, including sugar grams! Pretty sweet, huh? (The analysis, not the recipes!)

By the way, if you're one of the many Weight Watchers members who purchased our previous cookbooks and supported us by recommending our books on social media, I'd like to say a huge, heartfelt thank you.

This cookbook, my first solo effort, came to fruition while my *Looneyspoons* partner in crime and "twisted sister," Janet, was busy following her passion, which was pursuing a doctorate degree and wowing audiences with inspirational speaking gigs across the country. I'm so grateful that she gave me her blessing to follow my heart and make *Yum & Yummer* a reality. I'm pretty sure she was getting sick of me anyway. ☺ Sisters!

I hope you enjoy *Yum & Yummer* as much as I enjoyed creating it for you. I'm always here if you need me and I'll do my best to personally reply to every email (greta@yumyummer.com). Now go pick a recipe and get cooking!

Greta

The Videos

Yum & Yummer is the first cookbook EVER to include a 1-minute, upbeat, action-packed how-to video with every single recipe! Some book-marketing experts would call this "a digitally enhanced reader experience" but I just call it "super-cool bonus content!" Watching the videos is FUN and EASY! You'll notice a YUMcode (technically called a QR code but that's way too boring) on every recipe page. Just scan it using your smartphone or tablet (or watch all the videos online). I'm a technological idiot and I can do it—so you can, too! Trust me!

FROM YOUR SMARTPHONE OR TABLET

1. Open your app store (literally called App Store on an iPhone/iPad or Play Store on Android devices) and search for "QR code scanner." Dozens of FREE QR code scanner apps will appear.

2. Choose an app with high ratings and download it. It'll only take a minute.

3. Open your new QR code scanner app. The app will use your smartphone's camera to scan the code. Just point the camera at the YUMcode on any recipe page and ta-dah! The recipe video will magically appear! Isn't technology great?

4. Press play and crank up the volume!

Watch EVERY RECIPE come to life!

ONLINE

Visit my website yumyummer.com where you'll find every video for every recipe in this book in one neat and tidy place.

TIP: If you have any trouble understanding how to download an app or scan the YUMcodes, just ask your 11-year-old neighbor to help you out. ☺

Contents

CHAPTER 1

Snacketizers

Healthy snacks and appetizers
with serious yum factor!

YUM & YUMMER

Guac by Gretz*

Guacamole is quite possibly my favorite food. If I was shipped off to Siberia and only allowed to take one food item, it would be guacamole. Pretty sure if I had unlimited guacamole and L'Oréal Voluminous mascara, I'd survive just fine. Sometimes I eat only guacamole for dinner. With a spoon. Is that pathetic? Please don't tell anyone—people expect more from me!

3 large avocados (ripe but not squishy)

2 tbsp freshly squeezed lime juice

¾ tsp sea salt

1 cup finely diced Roma (plum)
   or grape tomatoes

½ cup finely minced red onions (fine!)

½ cup chopped fresh cilantro

1 small jalapeño pepper, finely minced

1 tsp minced garlic

¼ tsp ground cumin

Pinch cayenne pepper
   (or more if you like heat)

Note: Don't even dream of making guacamole with unripe avocados. Disaster.

* My nickname has been Gretz since I was a young girl. My teenage dream was to someday marry Wayne Gretzky so my name would be "Greta Gretzky." Kinda has a nice ring to it, right? No ring. No wedding. Sigh.

Peel and pit avocados. Scoop avocado flesh into a medium bowl. Add lime juice and salt. Using a potato masher, mash well but leave some lumps.

Add remaining ingredients and mix well. Cover with plastic wrap, pressing down lightly on the guacamole to create a tight, air-free seal. Refrigerate for 1 hour before serving.

Makes about 2½ cups guacamole

Per serving (¼ cup): 107 calories, 8.9 g total fat (1.3 g saturated fat), 1.6 g protein, 7.6 g carbohydrate (4.5 g fiber, 1.6 g sugars), 0 mg cholesterol, 165 mg sodium

SCAN FOR VIDEO!

ROCK SOME
Guac!

YUM
Omit the cumin and add
1 tsp dry taco seasoning.

YUMMER!
Cut carbs by serving
bunless burgers topped
with homemade guacamole.

Roasted Red Pepper Hummus

GF   DF   V

I once saw a bumper sticker that read "Real Women Love Hummus" and it made me laugh out loud because (1) it's SO TRUE, women go gaga for hummus, and (2) I happened to be eating hummus with a pen cap while driving behind aforementioned car bumper. I was starving, okay? And desperate, without any veggies or pita chips for dunking. Plus, it was roasted red pepper hummus, my favorite.

2 large red bell peppers

1 can (19 oz/540 mL) no-salt-added chickpeas, drained and rinsed

¼ cup tahini

¼ cup freshly squeezed lemon juice

2 tbsp olive oil

1 large clove garlic, smashed

½ tsp ground cumin

½ tsp sea salt

⅛ tsp smoked paprika (optional)

Move oven rack to top third of oven, so it's about 8 inches away from the broiler. Preheat the broiler to high.

Cut bell peppers in half lengthwise and remove seeds and stems. Place peppers cut-side down on a small baking sheet and flatten them with your hand. Broil peppers until skins are blistered and blackened, about 10 minutes or so. Carefully place the peppers in a glass bowl and cover tightly with plastic wrap. Let peppers steam for 15 minutes.

Peel off and discard blackened skin and place roasted peppers in the bowl of a food processor. (I save a quarter of a roasted pepper to chop and sprinkle on top. See photo.) Add all remaining ingredients and process until hummus is smooth and creamy.

For best flavor, refrigerate hummus for 2 to 3 hours before serving. Or, just start eating it with a spoon—whatever makes you happy.

Makes about 2½ cups dip

Per serving (2 tbsp): 74 calories, 4.3 g total fat (0.6 g saturated fat), 2.4 g protein, 7.2 g carbohydrate (1.8 g fiber, 1 g sugars), 0 mg cholesterol, 73 mg sodium

KITCHEN WHIZDOM

If you're like most people, you make hummus using canned chickpeas—and there's nothing wrong with that. Hummus aficionados SWEAR that soaking and cooking dried chickpeas results in a superior-tasting hummus, but I'm totally happy with my CANvenient method. That being said, here are five tricks for making the best-tasting hummus possible using freshly cooked OR canned chickpeas: (1) Fresh garlic, not powder. Ever. (2) Freshly squeezed lemon juice. Always. (3) Fat. Both good-quality olive oil and tahini are critical to creamy-tasting hummus. Don't skimp. Add more. Can't hurt. (4) A respectable food processor—for the smoothest consistency. Not a tiny one, either, where ingredients get jammed and the machine starts shrieking at you. (5) Time. As much as you'd like to dig right in, hummus tastes better after several hours of flavor-mingling in the fridge.

SCAN FOR VIDEO!

YUM
Sunflower butter is an excellent
substitute for tahini in hummus recipes.

YUMMER!
Try hummus instead of mayo
in egg-salad sandwich filling.

Tastier than STORE-BOUGHT!

⊰⊱ *Irresistibly Tasty* ⊰⊱
Maple-Cinnamon Roasted Chickpeas

A crunchy, high-fiber, protein-rich snack? Yes, peas! Roasting chickpeas with various oils and seasonings is certainly not a new idea, but I'm amazed at how many people have never tried them. Similar in texture to corn nuts…but they aren't corn OR nuts!

2 cans (19 oz/540 mL each) no-salt-added chickpeas, drained and rinsed

2 tbsp olive oil

¼ cup pure maple syrup

2 tsp ground cinnamon

½ tsp sea salt

¼ tsp cayenne pepper

Warning: If you aren't used to eating beans, go easy on these. Trust me. After all, they're beans… if you know what I mean. ☺

Makes about 2⅔ cups chickpeas

Per serving (⅓ cup): 175 calories, 5.2 g total fat (0.7 g saturated fat), 6 g protein, 26 g carbohydrate (4.2 g fiber, 7 g sugars), 0 mg cholesterol, 139 mg sodium

Preheat oven to 400°F. Line a large, rimmed baking sheet with foil or parchment paper and set aside.

After draining and rinsing the chickpeas, spread them out on a clean kitchen towel or paper towels. Pat dry using another towel or paper towels. Some skins will come loose as you dry the chickpeas. Pick them off and discard them (or they will burn during roasting). Do your best to dry the chickpeas without squishing them.

Transfer chickpeas to a medium mixing bowl. Add olive oil and toss until chickpeas are evenly coated with oil. Spread chickpeas in a single layer on prepared baking sheet. (They must be in a single layer or they will not roast properly.) Set bowl aside as you'll need it later. Roast chickpeas on middle oven rack for 30 minutes, stirring or jiggling the pan every 10 minutes or so to ensure even roasting.

Remove pan from oven. Reduce oven temperature to 325°F. Carefully pick up the parchment or foil and use it as a funnel to pour chickpeas back into mixing bowl. Add maple syrup, cinnamon, salt and cayenne pepper. Toss or mix with a spoon until chickpeas are evenly coated with seasonings. Return chickpeas to parchment- or foil-lined pan and spread out in a single layer. Roast for about 30 more minutes, being careful not to burn the chickpeas. Stir every 10 minutes to ensure even roasting.

Remove pan from oven and let chickpeas cool completely (at least 1 hour) before serving. They may seem chewy straight from the oven but will become crunchy when cooled. Store in a resealable bag or airtight container in the fridge for up to 2 days.

SCAN FOR VIDEO!

YUM

For a Tex-Mex variation, replace the cinnamon with 1½ tbsp dry taco seasoning (store-bought or homemade; see Kitchen Whizdom, page 38). Omit the sea salt and cayenne.

YUMMER!

Try roasted chickpeas as a healthy crouton replacement in salads.

TASTY

Sweet & Spicy
Apricot, Sriracha & Ginger-Glazed Meatballs

DF

As the saying goes, "These aren't your mama's meatballs!" Nothing against mama, of course. And I don't believe that's actually a saying. Regardless, I created this sweet-heat, party-meatball recipe specifically for Sriracha lovers. You know, the folks who carry around mini squeeze bottles of the trendy hot sauce on their key chains? Make these when you wanna kick things up a notch.

Meatballs

1½ lbs (680 g) lean ground chicken

½ cup dry unseasoned bread crumbs

¼ cup finely minced green onions
   (with white parts)

2 tbsp hoisin sauce

1 egg

2 tsp minced garlic

1 tsp grated fresh gingerroot

1 tsp dark sesame oil

½ tsp each sea salt and freshly ground
   black pepper

Glaze

1 cup no-sugar-added apricot jam*

¼ cup reduced-sodium soy sauce

1 tbsp freshly squeezed lime juice

1 tbsp Sriracha hot sauce

2 tsp minced garlic

2 tsp grated fresh gingerroot

½ tsp dark sesame oil

Finely chopped green onions and toasted
   sesame seeds for garnish (optional)

* I found three brands of no-sugar-added apricot jam at my grocery store, including the ubiquitous Smuckers.

Preheat oven to 400°F.

In a large bowl, combine ground chicken, bread crumbs, onions, hoisin sauce, egg, garlic, gingerroot, sesame oil, salt and pepper (using your hands works best). Form mixture into bite-sized meatballs, about 1½ inches in diameter. Wetting your hands helps prevent the chicken mixture from sticking to them. (Ground chicken and turkey are kinda sticky!) You should end up with about 40 meatballs.

Place meatballs on a non-stick baking sheet. Bake in preheated oven for 15 to 18 minutes or until cooked through. Stir meatballs once, halfway through cooking time, to brown sides.

While meatballs are cooking, prepare glaze. In a 10-inch, deep, non-stick skillet, whisk together jam, soy sauce, lime juice, Sriracha, garlic, gingerroot and sesame oil. Cook over medium-high heat until mixture is hot and bubbly and jam has melted. Add cooked meatballs and mix gently, ensuring every meatball is coated with sauce. Garnish with green onions and sesame seeds, if using. Serve hot.

Makes about 40 meatballs

Per meatball: 40 calories, 1.5 g total fat (0.4 g saturated fat), 3.6 g protein, 3.3 g carbohydrate (0 g fiber, 2.6 g sugars), 20 mg cholesterol, 121 mg sodium

SCAN FOR VIDEO!

YUM
For a faster version, use pre-made, frozen chicken or turkey meatballs.

YUMMER!
Let's make a meal! Serve these meatballs with Curried Coconut Rice (page 206) and a green veggie.

AMAZE BALLS

Fresh & Fabulous
Shrimp, Mango & Avocado Salad Cups

GF **DF**

Quick, simple and totally scrumptious, these adorable, colorful salad cups scream "summertime!"—yet you'll want to eat them all year round.

Dressing

2 tbsp olive oil

2 tbsp freshly squeezed lime juice

2 tsp liquid honey

1 tsp Dijon mustard

½ tsp grated lime zest

¼ tsp each sea salt and freshly ground black pepper

⅛ tsp each ground cumin and chili powder

Salad

1 lb (454 g) large cooked shrimp (25 to 30 per pound), chopped

2 medium mangos, cubed

1 large or 2 small avocados, cubed

1 cup peeled, diced English cucumbers

1 cup quartered grape tomatoes

⅔ cup chopped green onions

¼ cup chopped fresh cilantro

Whisk together all dressing ingredients in a small bowl or measuring cup. Refrigerate until ready to use.

Combine all salad ingredients in a large bowl. Mix gently to avoid mashing the avocados. Give dressing a quick whisk and add to salad. Mix gently until salad is coated with dressing. Add a bit more salt and pepper, if desired.

Divide salad among small cups (see photo) and serve with small spoons. May be served immediately or refrigerated until serving time.

Makes 8 servings

Per serving: 167 calories, 7.8 g total fat (1.2 g saturated fat), 13 g protein, 13 g carbohydrate (3 g fiber, 8 g sugars), 110 mg cholesterol, 215 mg sodium

These pretty salad cups look more appealing when you buy large shrimp and coarsely chop them. In other words, I don't recommend baby shrimp for this recipe. Make sure your mangos and avocados are ripe! Finally, don't prepare the salad too far in advance, since avocados turn brown so quickly. The fresher the salad, the better!

 SCAN FOR VIDEO!

SHRIMPLY IRRESISTIBLE!

YUM
Instead of mangos, try this salad with fresh peaches when they're in season.

YUMMER!
Serve as a main-course lunch or light dinner over your favorite greens. Makes 4 servings.

pumpkincredible

Combine 1½ cups plain hummus with ½ cup canned, pure pumpkin, 2 tsp pure maple syrup and ⅛ tsp ground cumin. Chill. Drizzle with pumpkin seed oil and top with toasted pumpkin seeds and a dash of smoked paprika.

lemon-DILLICIOUS

Combine 1½ cups plain hummus with 1 tbsp minced fresh dill and 1 tsp grated lemon zest. Chill.

sun-dried tomatOH!

Combine 1½ cups plain hummus with 3 tbsp sun-dried tomato pesto. Taste and add more pesto if desired. Chill. Drizzle lightly with good-quality olive oil before serving.

guacHUMole

Mash 1 medium ripe avocado with 1 tbsp freshly squeezed lime juice. Stir in 1 cup plain hummus and ¼ tsp each ground cumin and chili powder. Add a pinch of cayenne. Chill. Garnish with cilantro.

TURN HUMMUS into *Yummus!*

just *beet it!*

In the bowl of a mini food processor, whirl together 1½ cups plain hummus with 1 cup diced roasted golden beets, ¼ tsp ground cumin and ⅛ tsp curry powder until smooth. Chill.

See page 285 for Nutritional Info.

SCAN FOR VIDEO!

✦ The Lazy Gourmet's ✦
Butter Chicken Naan-Bread Pizzas

Who is the lazy gourmet? Me, when I'm tired and just don't feel like cooking. And probably you sometimes. Cooking from scratch day in and day out is challenging, so when I want gourmet flavor without all the work, I whip up these super-tasty, shortcut naan-bread pizzas and serve them in finger-food-sized wedges.

1 tbsp olive oil

1 lb (454 g) boneless skinless chicken breasts, cubed

1 cup butter chicken cooking sauce (see Kitchen Whizdom)

3 whole-grain naan flatbreads (4 to 5 oz/113 to 142 g each)

1 cup shredded Monterey Jack or mozzarella cheese* (4 oz/113 g)

1 cup diced fresh pineapple

⅓ cup red onion slivers (paper thin)

⅓ cup red bell pepper slivers (paper thin)

Minced fresh cilantro for garnish (optional but recommended)

* Use part-skim or regular cheese. You'll find some excellent pre-shredded blends at the grocery store and they're often on sale, which is *gouda* news, since cheese can be expensive.

Preheat oven to 400°F.

Heat olive oil in a 10-inch, non-stick skillet over medium-high heat. Add chicken cubes and cook until chicken is lightly browned and cooked through, about 5 to 7 minutes. Add butter chicken sauce. Mix well and reduce heat to medium-low. Cook and stir until mixture is hot and bubbly. Remove from heat and let mixture cool slightly. Sauce will thicken as it cools.

Spread saucy chicken evenly over naan bread. (If you like your pizza saucier, add a bit more sauce!) Sprinkle half the cheese over the chicken, followed by pineapple, onions and bell peppers. Top with remaining cheese.

Carefully slide pizzas directly onto middle oven rack. Bake for about 10 minutes, until crust is lightly browned and cheese is melted. Remove pizzas from oven, sprinkle with cilantro, if using, and serve hot.

Makes 6 servings

Per serving: 328 calories, 10.8 g total fat (3.9 g saturated fat), 28 g protein, 31 g carbohydrate (5 g fiber, 5.8 g sugars), 65 mg cholesterol, 475 mg sodium

As someone who cooks all the time, I welcome shortcuts, like buying prepared butter chicken sauce for this recipe. Tell me the truth: Would you actually take the time to prepare an entire butter chicken recipe from scratch, just to use a small portion of it for these pizzas? Didn't think so. And I'm pretty sure you don't have leftover butter chicken sitting around. Who EVER has leftover butter chicken? Is that even a thing? With the rise in popularity of Indian cooking, there are many brands of butter chicken cooking sauce to choose from. Check the sodium and fat content and decide which brand is best for you.

SCAN FOR VIDEO!

Wickedly Delicious
SPLURGE-WORTHY
Totally Worth It!

You'll wanna eat this NAAN-STOP!

Fruit & Feta Skewers with Mint
& Honey-Lime Balsamic Reduction

GF

Guests will happily devour the fruits of your (minimal) labor when you make these stunning watermelon, cucumber, feta and kiwi bites. The hint of honey and lime in the balsamic drizzle makes these mini, minty morsels taste marvelous!

Skewers

12 ¾-inch cubes seedless watermelon

12 fresh mint leaves

12 ¾-inch cubes peeled English cucumber

12 ¾-inch cubes light or regular feta cheese

12 ¾-inch cubes kiwi fruit

12 4-inch cocktail picks

Balsamic Reduction*

⅓ cup balsamic vinegar

1 tbsp liquid honey

1 tbsp freshly squeezed lime juice

Grated zest of 1 small lime

* Making your own balsamic reduction is easy, but if you'd rather buy it, I recommend Nonna Pia's brand.

Assemble the skewers in the following order: 1 watermelon cube, 1 mint leaf, 1 cucumber cube, 1 feta cube and 1 kiwi cube. Place skewers on a serving dish, cover with plastic wrap and refrigerate while you make the balsamic reduction.

Whisk together balsamic vinegar, honey and lime juice in your smallest pot or skillet over medium-high heat. When mixture comes to a boil, reduce heat immediately to a gentle simmer. Let the mixture simmer (not boil!) until it begins to get syrupy and reduces in quantity by about half, whisking occasionally. This should take no more than 5 minutes. It will coat the pan or skillet if you swirl it around. Remove from heat and stir in lime zest. Cool slightly before serving. It'll thicken a bit as it cools, so keep this in mind. If you accidentally thicken it too much, you can thin it with water.

Drizzle serving plate with 1 or 2 tbsp balsamic reduction and arrange skewers on top. Drizzle skewers with another 1 or 2 tbsp balsamic reduction. Serve immediately.

Makes 12 skewers

Per skewer: 67 calories, 2.9 g total fat (1.9 g saturated fat), 2.3 g protein, 8 g carbohydrate (0.9 g fiber, 6.1 g sugars), 11 mg cholesterol, 146 mg sodium

SCAN FOR VIDEO!

YUM
Use mini bocconcini instead of feta, basil instead of mint and lemon instead of lime.

YUMMER!
Save all the scraps from cubing the fruit and feta. Toss them in a bowl and drizzle with balsamic reduction for a sweet and savory salad.

EASY to *make*, HARD to *resist!*

Easy, Cheesy
Broccoli & Cheddar Quinoa Bites

GF

**If you love the taste of broccoli and cheddar soup, this recipe's for you!
Designed as a healthy snack for kids and baked in mini muffin cups, these blissful broccoli,
cheese and quinoa bites are the perfect size for little hands.**

2 cups cooked and cooled quinoa
   (see Kitchen Whizdom)

1 cup finely chopped broccoli florets

1 cup shredded old (sharp)
   cheddar cheese (part-skim
   or regular; 4 oz/113 g)

¼ cup freshly grated
   Parmesan cheese

2 eggs

½ tsp mustard powder

½ tsp sea salt

¼ tsp freshly ground black pepper

¼ tsp garlic powder

¼ tsp onion powder

Preheat oven to 350°F.

In a large bowl, combine quinoa, broccoli and both cheeses. Set aside.

In a small bowl, whisk together eggs, mustard powder, salt, pepper, garlic powder and onion powder. Pour egg mixture over quinoa mixture and stir until very well blended.

Lightly oil one 24-cup mini muffin tin or two 12-cup mini muffin tins (or spray with cooking spray). Spoon broccoli-quinoa mixture evenly into cups. Using the back of a small spoon, press down mixture so it's packed into cups.

Bake in preheated oven for 15 to 20 minutes, or until bites have firmed up and are golden brown around the edges. Remove from oven and let cool for 5 minutes before removing from pan. Serve warm.

Makes 24 bites

Per bite: 41 calories, 1.7 g total fat (0.8 g saturated fat), 2.5 g protein, 3.8 g carbohydrate (0.5 g fiber, 0.2 g sugars), 19 mg cholesterol, 92 mg sodium

I almost always cook quinoa in vegetable broth versus water to give it a flavor boost. You'll need about ⅔ cup dry quinoa + 1⅓ cups broth or water to get the 2 cups cooked quinoa called for in this recipe. When cooking quinoa, it's really important to give it time to "rest" before fluffing and serving (or using in recipes like this one). All that simmering is like an intense cardio workout for the quinoa and it desperately needs some recovery time! So, at the ending of cooking, remove the pot from the heat, leave the lid on and let the quinoa rest for a good 10 minutes. This resting time allows it to develop the perfect texture and prevents the dreaded soggy quinoa scenario that frustrated cooks have asked me about. For faster cooling, spread the quinoa on a baking sheet instead of leaving it in the pot.

SCAN FOR VIDEO!

Kid-approved!

Best-Ever Vietnamese Summer Rolls
with Peanut Dipping Sauce

I could eat freshly made summer rolls every day and never get tired of them. Practice makes perfect when it comes to rolling them, which might seem tricky at first. Speaking of perfect… the peanut sauce! This recipe is wordy, but worth the effort.

Peanut Dipping Sauce

⅓ cup natural peanut butter

3 tbsp HOT water

2 tbsp hoisin sauce*

2 tbsp freshly squeezed lime juice

1 tbsp reduced-sodium soy sauce*

2 tsp dark sesame oil

1 tsp minced garlic

1 tsp grated fresh gingerroot

1 tsp hot sauce (such as Sriracha) or
⅓ tsp crushed red pepper flakes (optional)

Summer Rolls

2 oz (57 g) rice vermicelli noodles, cooked
(optional)

1 tsp dark sesame oil

Small handful of fresh mint

8 large rice paper wrappers (about 8-inch
diameter)

½ large ripe mango, cut into julienne strips

½ large red bell pepper, cut into
julienne strips

½ large English cucumber, peeled
and cut into julienne strips

1 medium avocado, thinly sliced

½ cup chopped radicchio

Small handful of fresh cilantro

8 small, soft lettuce leaves (such as
Boston or butter lettuce)

Whisk together all sauce ingredients in a medium bowl until well blended. Set aside until ready to serve. The flavors will develop as it sits. Before assembling salad rolls, make sure everything is sliced and ready to go. If using vermicelli, coarsely chop the noodles and toss them with sesame oil.

Fill a large, shallow, 9-inch round cake pan or skillet with very hot water. (Keep some boiling water handy to add to the bowl as the water cools. The water must remain hot.) Working one at a time, soak rice papers in hot water for about 15 to 20 seconds, or until soft and pliable (time will vary with brand of rice paper). Transfer to a clean, plastic cutting board.

Place a few small mint leaves in center of wrapper and top with ⅛ noodles, if using, then three strips each of mango, bell peppers, cucumbers, avocados and radicchio. Add a few cilantro leaves and a small lettuce leaf. Fold bottom edge of rice paper up over filling and roll once to enclose. Fold in sides and continue to roll up tightly. If your rice paper rips, you soaked it too long. Try again!

Place rolls seam-side down on a plate and cover with a damp towel. Repeat process with remaining wrappers and veggies. Wrap tightly with plastic wrap and refrigerate until serving time. Serve with Peanut Dipping Sauce.

Makes 8 rolls

* For gluten-free peanut dipping sauce, use GF hoisin sauce and Tamari soy sauce.

Per roll (with ⅛ sauce): 199 calories, 9.5 g total fat (1.4 g saturated fat), 4.3 g protein, 26 g carbohydrate (2.6 g fiber, 4.7 g sugars), 0 mg cholesterol, 305 mg sodium

SCAN FOR VIDEO!

A handheld salad!

YUM
Can't have peanuts? Make the sauce with sunflower butter.

YUMMER!
Add two pieces of cooked shrimp per roll.

Roasted Sweet Potato & White Bean Dip

A delicious twist on traditional chickpea hummus, this simple bean dip gets a nutritious beta-carotene boost from the addition of luscious sweet potatoes.

2 cups peeled, diced sweet potatoes

2 large cloves garlic, peeled, left whole

2 tbsp olive oil, divided

1 can (19 oz/540 mL) no-salt-added white kidney or cannellini beans, drained and rinsed

3 tbsp tahini (see Kitchen Whizdom)

3 tbsp freshly squeezed lemon juice

1 tsp pure maple syrup

½ tsp each ground cumin and sea salt

¼ tsp freshly ground black pepper

⅛ tsp cayenne pepper

Preheat oven to 425°F.

In a small bowl, combine sweet potatoes, garlic cloves and 1 tbsp olive oil. Mix well. Transfer mixture to a small baking pan. Roast, uncovered, in preheated oven for about 20 minutes, until potatoes are tender. Stir occasionally to ensure even roasting. Remove from oven and let cool slightly.

Add roasted potatoes, garlic, remaining 1 tbsp olive oil and all remaining ingredients to the bowl of a food processor. Pulse on and off until mixture is smooth. Add water if necessary to achieve desired consistency.

Chill at least 3 hours before serving to let flavors develop. Serve with cucumber rounds, bell pepper strips, brown rice crackers or whole-grain pita wedges.

Makes about 3 cups dip

Per serving (2 tbsp): 52 calories, 2.3 g total fat (0.3 g saturated fat), 1.9 g protein, 6.4 g carbohydrate (1.6 g fiber, 0.8 g sugars), 0 mg cholesterol, 53 mg sodium

Tahini is a rich and creamy paste made from hulled, toasted sesame seeds and it adds a mild, nutty flavor to sauces, dips and dressings. Think peanut butter—only made with sesame seeds. Please don't leave it out of the recipe. Sunflower butter, found in the health-food aisle of most major grocery stores, is an excellent substitute for tahini in hummus recipes.

 SCAN FOR VIDEO!

NUTRISHALICIOUS!

YUMMER!
Serve with a drizzle of olive oil
and a light dusting of paprika.

YUM
Navy beans or chickpeas can be
used instead of the kidney beans.

❧ Cute & Crunchy ❧
Wonton Taco Cups

These tiny, tasty taco cups are nacho ordinary snack! The perfect "game day" finger food or Taco Tuesday dinner, these cute cups look fancy, but are actually quite easy to make. One bite and you'll be wonton some more!

48 wonton wrappers (3½-inch square)*

2 tsp olive oil

1 lb (454 g) extra-lean ground beef

1 tsp minced garlic

½ cup minced onions

½ cup minced green bell peppers

½ cup water

⅓ cup ketchup

3 tbsp taco seasoning (store-bought or homemade; see Kitchen Whizdom)

1 cup shredded old (sharp) cheddar cheese or Tex-Mex pre-shredded blend (part-skim or regular; 4 oz/113 g)

Toppings

Sour cream   **Guacamole**

Salsa   **Chopped green onions**

Fresh cilantro

* Look for wonton wrappers in the refrigerated section of most supermarket produce aisles.

Preheat oven to 375°F. Lightly oil two 12-cup muffin tins (or spray with cooking spray). Insert two wonton wrappers in each cup, overlapping them to make 8 points and pressing them down firmly (see video!). Bake wontons for about 8 minutes, until golden brown and lightly toasted. Be careful not to burn them. Remove from oven but keep oven on.

While wontons are baking, prepare filling. Heat olive oil in a medium skillet over medium-high heat. Add beef and garlic. Cook and stir until beef is no longer pink, breaking up any large pieces as it cooks. Add onions and bell peppers and cook for 3 more minutes. Add water, ketchup and taco seasoning. Mix well. Cook for 2 more minutes. Remove from heat.

Sprinkle 1 tsp cheese in bottom of cups, top with 1 tbsp beef filling, followed by another 1 tsp cheese. Return pans to oven and bake for 3 minutes, until cheese is completely melted. Serve immediately with your favorite taco toppings.

Makes 24 taco cups

Per cup (without toppings): 107 calories, 3.6 g total fat (1.5 g saturated fat), 6.9 g protein, 11.3 g carbohydrate (0.6 g fiber, 1.1 g sugars), 15 mg cholesterol, 215 mg sodium

When using prepared taco seasoning, choose the reduced-sodium variety. If you have a well-stocked spice rack (a healthy cooking must-have, in my opinion), it's super easy to make your own seasoning. Here's how you do it: In a small bowl, mix together 4 tsp chili powder, 1½ tsp ground cumin, 1 tsp paprika, 1 tsp sugar, ½ tsp seasoned salt, ½ tsp black pepper, ½ tsp garlic powder, ½ tsp ground coriander and ¼ tsp onion powder. This formula will make enough taco seasoning for this recipe, but you can double, triple or quadruple the recipe and store it in a small jar for use in other dishes.

SCAN FOR VIDEO!

salsa

green onions

sour cream

guac

cilantro

YUM
For vegetarian cups, use meat-free "crumbles" instead of beef.

YUMMER!
Use this filling for regular tacos served in soft, warm, 100% white-corn tortillas (gluten-free!).

CHAPTER 2

Raising the SALAD Bar

Take your salads to the next level with these gorgeous and gorge-worthy recipes!

YUM & YUMMER

Greek Lentil Salad

GF

If you're a fan of traditional Greek salad, you'll LOVE this high-fiber, high-protein version
featuring super-nutritious lentils. Anyone with a *pulse* should make it!
(Ha-ha! Sorry. They don't call me Greta PUNleski for nothing!)

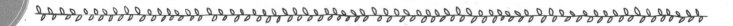

Salad

4 cups cooked brown lentils (or 2 cans,
  19 oz/540 mL each, drained and rinsed)

1½ cups quartered grape tomatoes

1½ cups peeled, diced English cucumbers

1 cup diced green bell peppers

¾ cup diced or very thinly sliced red onions

½ cup Kalamata olives

⅓ cup chopped fresh parsley

⅓ cup chopped fresh mint*

1 cup crumbled light or regular feta cheese
  (4 oz/113 g)

Dressing

3 tbsp olive oil

3 tbsp freshly squeezed lemon juice

1 tbsp apple cider vinegar

2 tsp liquid honey

1 tsp Dijon mustard

1 tsp minced garlic

½ tsp dried oregano

½ tsp each sea salt and freshly ground
  black pepper

In a large bowl, combine all salad ingredients and mix well.

Whisk together all dressing ingredients in a small bowl or measuring cup. Pour over salad and stir gently. Cover and refrigerate for at least 2 hours before serving.

* You can use fresh dill instead of mint, but reduce the amount to 3 tablespoons.

Makes about 9 cups salad

Per cup: 209 calories, 8.1 g total fat (1.9 g saturated fat), 11 g protein, 25 g carbohydrate (8.6 g fiber, 4 g sugars), 4 mg cholesterol, 413 mg sodium

SCAN FOR
VIDEO!

YUM
If you aren't looney for lentils like I am, use chickpeas.

YUMMER!
Feeling extra hungry? Serve this salad as a scrumptious side dish to grilled fish, chicken or steak.

One of my MOST REQUESTED salad recipes!

Super-Simple
Summery Chickpea Salad

GF DF V

It's the freshest, tastiest, easiest summer salad recipe. You can make it in minutes!
If you have tomatoes and cucumbers growing in your garden, now's the time to use them.
Interestingly, this super-healthy salad is my most-shared recipe EVER on Facebook!

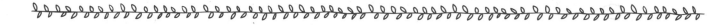

Salad

1 can (19 oz/540 mL) no-salt-added chickpeas,
   drained and rinsed
1½ cups peeled, diced English cucumbers
1½ cups halved grape tomatoes
¼ cup minced or thinly sliced red onions
1 medium avocado, diced

Dressing

2 tbsp freshly squeezed lemon juice
2 tbsp olive oil
1 tbsp balsamic vinegar
1 tbsp minced fresh dill
1 tsp Dijon mustard
1 tsp pure maple syrup or liquid honey
¼ tsp each sea salt and freshly ground
   black pepper

In a large bowl, combine all salad ingredients, being careful not to squish the avocados.

Whisk together all dressing ingredients in a small bowl or measuring cup. Pour over salad and mix well. Taste and add more salt and pepper if you like. Serve immediately.

Makes about 6 cups salad

Per cup: 184 calories, 9.5 g total fat (1.3 g saturated fat), 5.5 g protein, 21 g carbohydrate (5.2 g fiber, 4 g sugars), 0 mg cholesterol, 116 mg sodium

SCAN FOR VIDEO!

YUM
Try lime juice and cilantro instead of lemon juice and dill.

YUMMER!
Many Facebook fans suggested adding crumbled feta to the mix. Go for it!

Tex-Mex Quinoa Salad
with Chili-Lime Dressing

(GF) (DF) (V)

**Serve this flavor-packed, high-fiber, low-sodium salad as a sensational side dish
to any grilled meats or by itself as a satisfying lunch.**

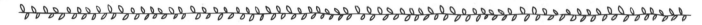

Salad

1 cup uncooked quinoa (see Kitchen Whizdom)

1¾ cups reduced-sodium vegetable broth

1 cup quartered grape tomatoes

1 cup no-salt-added canned black beans,
   drained and rinsed

1 cup whole-kernel corn

1 cup diced orange bell peppers

½ cup chopped green onions (with white parts)

1 small jalapeño pepper, very finely minced

2 to 3 tbsp minced fresh cilantro

1 medium avocado, diced

Dressing

3 tbsp freshly squeezed lime juice

2 tbsp olive oil or avocado oil

2 tsp liquid honey (use pure maple syrup for vegan)

½ tsp each ground cumin and chili powder

¼ tsp freshly ground black pepper

In a medium pot, combine quinoa and vegetable broth. Bring to a boil over high heat. Reduce heat to low, cover and simmer for 12 to 15 minutes, or until quinoa is tender and broth has been absorbed. Remove from heat and let stand, covered, for 10 minutes. Cool completely.

Transfer cooled quinoa to a large bowl. Add tomatoes, beans, corn, bell peppers, onions, jalapeño and cilantro. Mix well.

Whisk together all dressing ingredients in a small bowl or measuring cup. Pour over salad and mix well. Cover and refrigerate for at least 4 hours. Add diced avocados just before serving.

Makes 8 cups salad

Per cup: 212 calories, 8.3 g total fat (0.9 g saturated fat), 4.9 g protein, 30 g carbohydrate (6.8 g fiber, 3.9 g sugars), 0 mg cholesterol, 138 mg sodium

KITCHEN WHIZDOM

When making quinoa salad, I like to use a combination of white and red quinoa so the salad looks prettier. My preferred ratio is two parts white to one part red. If your quinoa isn't the pre-rinsed variety (check the bag or box), then place it in a mesh sieve and rinse it well under cold running water before cooking. Rinsing removes quinoa's natural coating, called saponin, which can make it taste bitter or soapy.

SCAN FOR VIDEO!

Grilling the corn
MAKES IT EVEN TASTIER!

Winter Grain Salad
with Roasted Squash, Pomegranate, Feta & Mint

GF*

Nothing like a little *cucurbita moschata* (butternut squash) to jazz up a grain salad! This hearty and healthy recipe isn't just pretty to look at, it's pretty tasty, too. As much as I love and crave salads, sometimes leafy green ones just don't cut it in the fall or winter. That's when this salad comes to the rescue.

Salad

4 cups cubed butternut squash
   (about ½-inch cubes)

1 tbsp olive oil

4 cups cooked, cooled grains
   (see Kitchen Whizdom)

1 cup pomegranate seeds

⅓ cup chopped green onions (with white parts)

⅓ cup chopped fresh parsley

⅓ cup chopped fresh mint

⅓ cup crumbled light or regular feta cheese
   (1½ oz/43 g)

Dressing

2 tbsp olive oil

2 tbsp freshly squeezed lemon juice

1 tbsp pure maple syrup or liquid honey

2 tsp balsamic vinegar (white or regular)

1 tsp Dijon mustard

½ tsp grated orange zest (optional but nice)

Sea salt and freshly ground black pepper

* For gluten-free, grains like quinoa, brown rice and wild rice
(or a combo) would be perfect.

Preheat oven to 400°F. Toss squash cubes with 1 tbsp olive oil and a sprinkle of salt and pepper. Spread squash evenly on a small, parchment-lined baking sheet. Roast for about 20 minutes. Give squash a stir halfway through cooking time. Squash should be tender but still have a slight bite. Squishy squash is not good! Remove from oven and let cool.

In a large bowl, combine cooked grains, squash, pomegranate, green onions, parsley, mint and feta. Stir gently to combine. Pretty!

Whisk together all dressing ingredients, except salt and pepper. Pour over salad. Add salt and pepper to taste. A generous grinding of both. Mix well, being careful not to squish the squash. Cover with plastic wrap and refrigerate until chilled. This salad also tastes great at room temperature.

Makes about 8 cups salad

Per cup: 231 calories, 7.8 g total fat (1.7 g saturated fat), 6 g protein, 36 g carbohydrate (5.3 g fiber, 6.8 g sugars), 2 mg cholesterol, 256 mg sodium

You can use just about any grain you prefer in this salad: red and/or white quinoa (technically a seed), wheat berries, farro, bulgur, brown and wild rice, mix a bunch together, use couscous…whatever! Just make sure you use 4 cups (or so) of COOKED grains and let them cool after cooking. Can't find pomegranate at the store? Use dried cranberries. Not a fan of squash? Use sweet potatoes.

SCAN FOR VIDEO!

Roasted butternut squash makes this salad "gourd"ious!

Chicken BLT Pasta Salad
with Creamy Poppy Seed Dressing

This crowd-pleasing salad has Father's Day BBQ, long-weekend cookout or summer potluck party written all over it! Chicken. Pasta. Bacon. Creamy dressing. Need I say more?
Yup: It's wickedly delicious and totally worth it!

Dressing

1 recipe Creamy Poppy Seed Dressing (page 56)

Salad

1 pkg (13 oz/375 g) uncooked rotini (regular, whole wheat or gluten-free)

2 cups chopped Romaine hearts or chopped baby spinach

2 cups chopped cooked chicken breast

1 cup halved or quartered grape tomatoes or chopped Roma (plum) tomatoes

8 slices nitrate-free bacon, cooked and chopped

¾ cup frozen green peas, thawed

½ cup chopped green onions

Freshly ground black pepper to taste

Make the dressing and store it in the fridge until you're ready to use it.

Cook rotini according to package directions. Drain, rinse with cold water (to stop the cooking action) and drain again. Transfer rotini to a very large bowl.

Add all remaining salad ingredients to cooked rotini and mix well. Add the prepared dressing (all of it) and mix again, until all ingredients are well coated. Serve immediately. See Kitchen Whizdom for make-ahead tips.

Makes 10 generous cups salad

Per cup: 306 calories, 12.3 g total fat (2 g saturated fat), 16.5 g protein, 30.6 g carbohydrate (4.4 g fiber, 3.6 g sugars), 76 mg cholesterol, 255 mg sodium

If preparing this salad in advance, add the dressing and greens (lettuce or spinach) just before serving. Otherwise, the noodles will soak up all the dressing and the lettuce will be wilty and wimpy. You don't want that! I prefer the fat, plump rotini noodles in this salad versus the skinny, no-personality, rotini-wannabe fusilli. Rotini was perfectly designed by the Italians to hold sauces and dressings better than most pasta shapes.

SCAN FOR VIDEO!

SPLURGE-WORTHY

Wickedly Delicious

Totally Worth It!

YUM Not crazy about poppy seed dressing? Use ranch or Caesar dressing instead.

YUMMER! Shredded sharp cheddar makes it even beddar! But don't go crazy, please. The salad's already pretty decadent. ☺

Chicken & Mango Salad
~ with Sesame-Ginger Dressing ~

My love of mangos was solidified when, while vacationing in Costa Rica, a ripe mango fell from a tree and hit me square on the head. It was the tastiest, sweetest, most perfect mango I'd ever eaten. In Isaac-Newton-like fashion, this fruitful event sparked a "Eureka!" recipe moment that led to the creation of this mango-licious chicken salad.

Sesame-Ginger Dressing

¼ cup neutral-tasting oil, such as sunflower
   or safflower oil (I use organic)

3 tbsp seasoned rice vinegar

2 tbsp dark sesame oil

1 tbsp liquid honey

1 tbsp reduced-sodium soy sauce
   (use Tamari soy sauce for gluten-free)

2 tsp grated fresh gingerroot

1 tsp minced garlic

¼ tsp sea salt

⅛ tsp crushed red pepper flakes (optional)

Salad

1 large ripe mango, peeled and thinly sliced

1 large red bell pepper, thinly sliced

1 cup packed grated carrots

½ cup very thinly sliced red onions

⅓ cup coarsely chopped cilantro (or mint)

6 cups packed mixed greens

3 cooked medium chicken breasts, thinly sliced
   or chopped

Chopped cashews, peanuts or sesame seeds
   for garnish (optional)

Whisk together all dressing ingredients in a small bowl or measuring cup. Refrigerate until ready to use. For a "creamier," smoother dressing, whirl all dressing ingredients in a small blender (such as a Ninja, Magic Bullet, etc.) for about 10 seconds.

In a large bowl, combine mangos, bell peppers, carrots, onions and cilantro. Mix well. Add 3 tbsp dressing and mix again (using tongs works well).

Arrange greens over bottom of 6 serving plates or bowls. Mound mango mixture on greens. Top with sliced chicken. Drizzle more dressing over the chicken. You might not use all of it. Garnish with chopped cashews, if using, and serve immediately. (Alternatively, you can toss everything together in a large bowl: the mango mixture, greens, chicken, dressing and nuts, or arrange individual salads as in photo and serve the dressing on the side. I used a spiralizer to make the carrots curly!)

Makes 6 servings

Per serving: 282 calories, 16 g total fat (1.9 g saturated fat), 17 g protein, 21 g carbohydrate (3.6 g fiber, 15 g sugars), 40 mg cholesterol, 243 mg sodium

SCAN FOR VIDEO!

TRY THIS DRESSING
AS A MARINADE FOR
salmon!

YUM For a vegan option, replace the chicken with sliced avocados and the honey with maple syrup or your sweetener of choice.

YUMMER! For a slightly thicker, richer dressing, add a tablespoon of peanut butter, almond butter or sunflower butter.

Crunchy Asian Slaw

GF* DF V

**Lots of texture and beautiful colors make this delicious salad a feast for your eyes
AND your taste buds!**

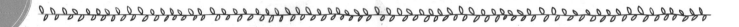

Salad

4 cups packed chopped Napa cabbage**

1½ cups grated or finely sliced red cabbage

1½ cups grated carrots

1 cup finely diced red bell peppers

1 cup julienned snow peas or sugar snap peas

½ cup chopped green onions

½ cup chopped peanuts

¼ cup chopped fresh cilantro

2 tbsp toasted sesame seeds (optional)

Dressing

¼ cup hoisin sauce*

2 tbsp sunflower or peanut oil

2 tbsp dark sesame oil

2 tbsp freshly squeezed lime juice

2 tbsp rice vinegar

1 tbsp grated fresh gingerroot

1 tsp minced garlic

**Pinch crushed red pepper flakes
   (or a few drops hot sauce)**

Sea salt and freshly ground black pepper to taste

In a large bowl, combine all salad ingredients and mix well. Set aside.

Whisk together all dressing ingredients in a small bowl or measuring cup. Pour over salad. Mix well using tongs. Make sure salad is evenly coated with dressing. You can serve it immediately or cover and refrigerate until serving time. (Give the salad a good toss before serving if it's been sitting in the fridge.)

Makes 8 side-dish servings

Per serving: 142 calories, 10 g total fat (1.4 g saturated fat), 3 g protein, 11 g carbohydrate (3 g fiber, 6.1 g sugars), 0 mg cholesterol, 155 mg sodium

* If gluten-free is important to you, look for gluten-free hoisin sauce. The popular Lee Kum Kee brand now makes a GF version plus there are several brands available online.

** You can replace the Napa cabbage and red cabbage with bagged coleslaw mix. Look for interesting blends of "slaw mix" in the produce section of your grocery store. I like mixes that include green and red cabbage, carrots, kale and Brussels sprouts.

SCAN FOR VIDEO!

YUM Add sliced almonds or chopped cashews instead of peanuts.

YUMMER! Serve with Roasted Asian Salmon Fillets, page 128.

Try adding shaved Brussels sprouts to any coleslaw recipe.

Creamy Poppy Seed

Per tablespoon: 51 calories, 4.3 g total fat (0.4 g saturated fat), 0.8 g protein, 1.3 g carbohydrate (0.1 g fiber, 0.8 g sugars), 2.6 mg cholesterol, 78 mg sodium

½ cup mayonnaise
½ cup plain 0% Greek yogurt
1½ tbsp white wine vinegar
1 tbsp freshly
squeezed lemon juice
1 tbsp sugar or liquid honey
2 tsp poppy seeds
½ tsp mustard powder
¼ tsp sea salt
⅛ tsp freshly ground
black pepper

Makes just over 1 cup dressing

Pomegranate Balsamic

Per tablespoon: 66 calories, 7 g total fat (1 g saturated fat), 0 g protein, 1.8 g carbohydrate (0 g fiber, 1.5 g sugars), 0 mg cholesterol, 41 mg sodium

½ cup olive oil
¼ cup pomegranate juice*
3 tbsp balsamic vinegar
1 tsp Dijon mustard
2 tsp pure maple syrup or
liquid honey
1 tsp minced garlic or 1 tbsp
minced shallots
¼ tsp each sea salt and
freshly ground black pepper

* I use POM Wonderful brand.

Makes about 1 cup dressing

LEMON-TAHINI

Per tablespoon: 71 calories, 6.7 g total fat (1 g saturated fat), 0.7 g protein, 2.9 g carbohydrate (0.4 g fiber, 1.8 g sugars), 0 mg cholesterol, 64 mg sodium

¼ cup olive oil
¼ cup freshly squeezed
lemon juice
3 tbsp tahini
1 to 2 tbsp pure maple syrup
1 tsp reduced-sodium soy sauce
(use Tamari soy sauce
for gluten-free)
¼ tsp each sea salt and freshly
ground black pepper

For a thinner consistency,
add a bit of warm water.

Makes about ¾ cup dressing

SCAN FOR VIDEO!

The Best Dressed

Making healthy, homemade salad dressings is ridiculously easy!

Citrus Vinaigrette GF DF

Per tablespoon: 58 calories, 6 g total fat (0.9 g saturated fat), 0 g protein, 1.9 g carbohydrate (0 g fiber, 1.6 g sugars), 0 mg cholesterol, 63 mg sodium

DIRECTIONS FOR ALL DRESSINGS:

Whisk together all ingredients in a small bowl or measuring cup until well blended. Or, place all ingredients in a Mason jar and shake well. Store in the fridge for up to 5 days.

½ cup olive oil
¼ cup freshly squeezed orange juice
¼ cup white balsamic vinegar
2 tbsp freshly squeezed lemon juice
1 tbsp liquid honey
1 tbsp finely minced shallots
1 tsp Dijon mustard
½ tsp sea salt
¼ tsp freshly ground black pepper

Makes just over 1 cup dressing

Galas, Greens & Gorgonzola

Thinly sliced Gala apples with mixed greens, shaved Brussels sprouts, maple-roasted pecans and mild blue cheese, topped with a lip-smackin', plate-lickin' white balsamic vinaigrette. Yes, please! Make this impressive salad when company's coming.

White Balsamic Vinaigrette

¼ cup olive oil

2 tbsp white balsamic vinegar

1 tbsp freshly squeezed lemon juice

2 tsp pure maple syrup or liquid honey

½ tsp Dijon mustard

½ tsp minced garlic

¼ tsp each sea salt and freshly ground black pepper

Salad

6 cups packed mixed greens

1½ cups very thinly sliced (shaved) raw Brussels sprouts

1 large Gala apple, unpeeled, cored and thinly sliced

½ cup crumbled Gorgonzola (or feta) cheese (about 2 oz/57 g)

½ cup maple-roasted pecans (recipe below)

Whisk together all vinaigrette ingredients in a small bowl or measuring cup. Refrigerate until ready to use. (Whisk again before drizzling on salad.)

Just before serving, place greens, Brussels sprouts, apples and cheese in a very large salad bowl. Add dressing and toss or mix well (I use tongs) until all greens are well coated. Top individual servings with roasted pecans. I like to chop or crumble them a bit before sprinkling them on my salad. So tasty!

Makes 6 servings

Per serving: 229 calories, 18 g total fat* (3.4 g saturated fat), 4 g protein, 16 g carbohydrate (4.4 g fiber, 8.5 g sugars), 9 mg cholesterol, 300 mg sodium

* Most of the fat comes from olive oil and nuts…a bit from the cheese, too, but mostly good fats in this salad!

To make maple-roasted pecans, preheat oven to 325°F and line your smallest baking pan with parchment paper. In a medium bowl, combine 1½ cups pecan halves, 2 tbsp maple syrup, 1 tbsp melted butter or coconut oil, ½ tsp ground cinnamon and ¼ tsp sea salt. Stir until well blended. Spread coated pecans in a single layer on the parchment-lined pan. Bake for 10 minutes, give pecans a quick stir, then bake an additional 7 to 10 minutes. Be careful not to burn them. Let cool completely. Use ½ cup (or more!) roasted pecans in the salad and save the rest for a snack.

SCAN FOR VIDEO!

YUM Use your favorite variety of apple (or pear!) in this recipe.

YUMMER! Throw in some red onion slivers and dried cranberries to make it extra fancy-schmancy.

Impossibly Delicious
Quinoa Tabbouleh Salad

Traditional Middle Eastern tabbouleh gets a modern upgrade when "superfood" quinoa replaces the usual cracked bulgur wheat. Serve it with grilled kabobs, hummus and pitas, or alone as a salad. Fresh and delish!

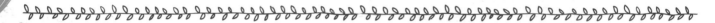

Salad

1 cup uncooked quinoa, rinsed (white, red or a combination of both)

1¾ cups reduced-sodium vegetable broth

½ tsp ground cumin

1 cup peeled, finely diced English cucumbers

1 cup quartered grape tomatoes

½ cup each finely grated carrots and chopped green onions

½ cup pomegranate seeds

½ cup chopped fresh parsley

⅓ cup chopped fresh mint

Dressing

2 tbsp olive oil

2 tbsp freshly squeezed lemon juice

1 tsp grated lemon zest

1 tsp mined garlic

½ tsp each sea salt and freshly ground black pepper

In a medium pot, combine quinoa, vegetable broth and cumin. Bring to a boil. Reduce heat to low, cover and simmer for 12 to 15 minutes, or until quinoa is tender and liquid has been absorbed. Remove from heat and let stand, covered, for 10 minutes. Cool completely. (Spread cooked quinoa on a baking sheet to speed up the cooling process.)

Transfer cooled quinoa to a mixing bowl. Add cucumbers, tomatoes, carrots, green onions, pomegranate, parsley and mint. Mix well.

Whisk together olive oil, lemon juice, lemon zest and garlic in a small bowl or measuring cup. Pour over salad. Mix well. Add salt and pepper and mix again. Cover and refrigerate for several hours for the best flavor.

Makes about 6 cups salad

Per cup: 147 calories, 6.3 g total fat (0.7 g saturated fat), 4 g protein, 21 g carbohydrate (3 g fiber, 1.3 g sugars), 0 mg cholesterol, 238 mg sodium

Have you ever made quinoa in a Thermos? You gotta try it! Here's my no-fail, no-burn, overnight Thermos method for perfectly cooked quinoa: Put 1 cup uncooked quinoa in a high-quality Thermos. Add 1¾ cups BOILING water, vegetable broth or chicken broth. Close lid tightly. Gently tilt Thermos back and forth a couple times to mix contents. Go to bed. Dream about George Clooney. Wake up to perfectly cooked, fluffy quinoa! Important: Don't use a cheap Thermos that doesn't retain heat well. The Thermos I use is a metal, 24-oz "wide mouth" type. I see them everywhere for around $30. It's worth the money to own a good Thermos. Don't use a super-tall Thermos or you'll never get the quinoa out of it. Speaking from experience here.

SCAN FOR VIDEO!

LIGHT & LEMONY

My "Famous"
Kaleslaw Salad

GF DF V

Why is this recipe famous? Because it's the most popular, most requested, most talked about kale salad recipe ever! Or, at least it seems like it. I can't take it anywhere without someone demanding or begging for the recipe. I personally make this salad more than any other in this book…and I eat A LOT of salads! Even my "Yuck-I'm-NEVER-eating-disgusting-kale" boyfriend loves it. And I'm pretty sure you will, too.

Apple Cider Vinaigrette

⅓ cup olive oil

3 tbsp apple cider vinegar

2 tbsp freshly squeezed lemon juice

2 tbsp Dijon mustard

2 tbsp pure maple syrup

¼ tsp each sea salt and freshly ground
   black pepper (or to taste)

Salad

4 cups packed chopped kale (ribs removed)

2 cups finely sliced or grated red cabbage

2 cups grated carrots

1 cup dried cranberries

¾ cup pumpkin seeds

½ cup chopped green onions (with white parts)

⅓ cup chopped fresh parsley

Whisk together all dressing ingredients in a small bowl or measuring cup. Set aside until ready to use.

Place chopped kale in a large bowl. Add ¼ cup vinaigrette and massage kale for 5 minutes using your hands. I know this is weird and cumbersome but just do it, please. ☺ You'll thank me later.

Add all remaining salad ingredients and at least 6 tbsp dressing (or more, if desired; you might not use all of it). Mix well. Cover and refrigerate for at least 1 hour before serving.

Makes about 8 cups salad

Per cup: 229 calories, 12.9 g total fat (2.2 g saturated fat), 5.8 g protein, 27 g carbohydrate (3.8 g fiber, 14.7 g sugars*), 0 mg cholesterol, 154 mg sodium

* Reduce the sugar content by using reduced-sugar Craisins (50% less sugar than regular Craisins).

SCAN FOR VIDEO!

YUM
Sliced almonds are a tasty substitution for the pumpkin seeds.

YUMMER!
Add one large, unpeeled, diced apple. Delicious! (Delicious as in "yummy." Not as in "Delicious apple." However, a Delicious apple would be great!)

Frugalicious
Lentil & Black Bean Salad

Potluck coming up? This high-fiber, high-protein salad always gets high praise from taste testers! You'll make everyone happy, too, since it's vegan AND gluten-free. I love that it's super simple to make and lasts for days in the fridge. Cheap and easy! Gotta love that!

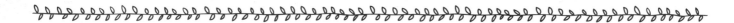

Salad

1 can (19 oz/540 mL) lentils, drained and rinsed

1 can (19 oz/540 mL) no-salt-added black beans, drained and rinsed

1 can (14 oz/398 mL) whole-kernel corn, drained

1 cup diced red bell peppers

¾ cup each diced celery and green bell peppers

½ cup chopped green onions

¼ cup chopped fresh parsley

Dressing

¼ cup olive oil or good-quality vegetable oil

3 tbsp red wine vinegar

1 tbsp freshly squeezed lemon juice

1 tbsp liquid honey (use pure maple syrup for vegan)

½ tsp Dijon mustard

Sea salt and freshly ground black pepper to taste

In a large bowl, combine all salad ingredients. Be careful not to squish the beans and lentils.

Whisk together all dressing ingredients in a small bowl or measuring cup. Pour over salad and mix well. Add several grinds of black pepper and a pinch or two of sea salt and mix again. Refrigerate for at least 4 hours before serving. (Tastes even better if made 1 day ahead. I know, that's a long time to wait!)

Makes about 10 cups salad

Per cup: 186 calories, 6.6 g total fat (0.9 g saturated fat), 8 g protein, 26 g carbohydrate (7 g fiber, 4 g sugars), 0 mg cholesterol, 154 mg sodium

Buy no-salt-added beans and lentils to keep the sodium count low. If you can't find the reduced-sodium variety, make sure you drain and rinse them well. I often use organic sunflower or safflower oil in this recipe and other dressings that benefit from a neutral-tasting oil.

SCAN FOR VIDEO!

8 g protein, 7 g fiber per cup. Wow!

California Quinoa Salad

(My Whole Foods copycat recipe)

GF DF V

I love shopping at Whole Foods and I particularly like their California Quinoa Salad, which you'll find on their spectacular salad bar. The flavors, the colors, the crunch! Sadly, the closest Whole Foods is an hour-long drive from my house. Naturally, this meant I had to create my own version of their irresistible salad.

Salad

1 cup uncooked quinoa, rinsed*

1¾ cups water

1 cup diced ripe mangos

¾ cup frozen shelled edamame beans, thawed

¾ cup diced red bell peppers

½ cup sliced almonds

⅓ cup raisins

⅓ cup finely minced red onions

⅓ cup unsweetened flaked coconut

3 tbsp minced fresh cilantro

Dressing

2 tbsp olive oil

2 tbsp freshly squeezed lime juice

1 tbsp balsamic vinegar (white or regular)

2 tsp liquid honey (use pure maple syrup for vegan)

Sea salt and freshly ground black pepper to taste

* I use ⅔ cup white quinoa + ⅓ cup red quinoa in this recipe.

In a medium pot, combine quinoa and water. Bring to a boil over high heat. Reduce heat to low, cover and simmer for 12 to 15 minutes, or until quinoa is tender and water has been absorbed. Remove from heat and let stand, covered, for 10 minutes. Cool completely.

In a large bowl, stir together cooled quinoa, mangos, edamame, bell peppers, almonds, raisins, onions, coconut and cilantro. Set aside.

In a small bowl, whisk together olive oil, lime juice, vinegar and honey. Pour over salad and mix well. Add salt and pepper to taste and mix again. Chill until cold.

Makes 6 cups salad

Per cup: 269 calories, 13 g total fat (3 g saturated fat), 7 g protein, 34 g carbohydrate (4.6 g fiber, 13.7 g sugars), 0 mg cholesterol, 101 mg sodium

SCAN FOR VIDEO!

Perfect for potlucks

YUM
Sub green peas for
the edamame beans
and fresh mint for the cilantro.
Not a fan of mango? No problem!
Use diced peaches or nectarines.

YUMMER!
Cook the quinoa in vegetable broth instead of water for a flavor boost.

Sensational Spinach Salad
with Chicken, Strawberries & Avocados

GF DF

I often blend spinach, strawberries and avocados in my healthy morning smoothies, and that inspired me to create this beautiful, simple, early summer salad (when strawberries are tastiest!). I never, ever get tired of eating it. So delicious and so gorgeous!

Dressing

¼ cup light-tasting olive oil

¼ cup freshly squeezed orange juice

2 tbsp freshly squeezed lemon juice

2 tbsp Dijon mustard

1 tbsp apple cider vinegar

1 tbsp liquid honey

1 tsp each grated orange zest and grated
   fresh gingerroot (do not use dried)

¼ tsp each sea salt and freshly ground
   black pepper

2 tsp poppy seeds

Salad

1 container (5 oz/142 g) fresh baby spinach

2 cups sliced fresh strawberries (the fresher,
   the better!)

2 cups chopped cooked chicken breast

1 cup peeled, diced English cucumbers

1 large avocado, diced

⅓ cup sliced almonds (lightly toasted if possible)

⅓ cup very thinly sliced red onions

Add all dressing ingredients except poppy seeds to a blender and whirl until emulsified. A small, Magic Bullet-type blender works great for this purpose. Stir in poppy seeds and refrigerate until serving time. Give the dressing a good stir/shake/whisk before using.

Place all salad ingredients in a large bowl. Add half the dressing and mix gently with tongs, being careful not to squish the avocados. Add more dressing if needed and serve immediately.

Note: You can layer a smaller version of this salad in a Mason jar to take to work for lunch!

Makes 6 servings

Per serving: 275 calories, 18.7 g total fat (2.9 g saturated fat), 15.4 g protein, 15 g carbohydrate (4 g fiber, 8 g sugars), 32 mg cholesterol, 238 mg sodium

SCAN FOR VIDEO!

YUM Use half baby spinach leaves and half baby kale leaves.

YUMMER! Sprinkle some crumbled feta cheese over the salad before serving.

Spinach

Avocados

Strawberries

Almonds

Chicken

Red Onions

Cucumbers

Dressing

Strawberry & Watermelon Salad
with Feta, Mint & Honey-Lime Dressing

GF

Sometimes simple can be simply amazing! Crisp, cool and refreshing watermelon pairs perfectly with juicy strawberries and tangy lime juice. Chunks of feta and sprigs of fresh mint take it over the top. Easy-peasy, summer breezy!

Salad

3 cups sliced or chopped strawberries

3 cups cubed seedless watermelon (½-inch cubes)

1 cup peeled, diced English cucumbers

½ cup very thinly sliced red onions

⅓ cup chopped fresh mint

1 cup diced light or regular feta cheese (4 oz/113 g)

Dressing

2 tbsp olive oil

2 tbsp freshly squeezed lime juice

1 tbsp liquid honey

¼ tsp each sea salt and freshly ground
   black pepper

In a large bowl, combine all salad ingredients except feta cheese. Mix gently.

Whisk together all dressing ingredients in a small bowl or measuring cup. Pour over salad. Mix gently to coat salad with dressing. Add feta cheese and mix again. Serve immediately.

Makes about 8 cups salad

Per cup: 112 calories, 5.7 g total fat (1.8 g saturated fat), 4 g protein, 14 g carbohydrate (2.3 g fiber, 9 g sugars), 5 mg cholesterol, 272 mg sodium

KITCHEN WHIZDOM

This salad tastes best when prepared right before serving. It doesn't keep well in the fridge and will become mushy if made in advance. It's best to dice the feta cheese with a knife rather than crumble it into fine pieces. Tiny pieces of feta (crumbs) make the salad look unattractive. The strawberries and watermelon will stain the feta pink if mixed too far in advance. Soak the red onion slices in ice-cold water for 10 minutes to reduce their "sharpness." Don't like cucumbers? Try diced honeydew melon.

SCAN FOR VIDEO!

Summer in a bowl

CHAPTER 3

Spoons
&
SWOONS

Soups and chilis that'll bowl you over!

YUM & YUMMER

Lemon Chicken & Orzo Soup

DF

It's a comforting bowl of chicken soup for the soul. I love the hint of lemony, refreshing goodness that sets this soup apart from traditional chicken soup. Rice-shaped orzo pasta subs perfectly in place of boring, ordinary soup noodles. Need a gluten-free option? Use rice instead of orzo (you'll need to simmer it a bit longer).

1 tbsp olive oil

1½ cups chopped onions

1 cup each diced carrots and diced celery

1 tsp minced garlic

1 tsp dried thyme

½ tsp each dried marjoram and dried tarragon

¼ tsp ground turmeric (optional, for color)

6 cups reduced-sodium chicken broth

¼ cup freshly squeezed lemon juice

2 bay leaves

2 tsp grated lemon zest

½ tsp sea salt

¼ tsp freshly ground black pepper

½ cup uncooked orzo pasta

2 cups chopped cooked chicken
   (see Kitchen Whizdom)

¼ cup chopped fresh parsley

Heat olive oil in a large soup pot over medium heat. Add onions, carrots, celery and garlic. Cook and stir until vegetables begin to soften, about 5 minutes.

Add thyme, marjoram, tarragon and turmeric, if using. Mix well. Add broth, lemon juice, bay leaves, lemon zest, salt and pepper. Bring soup to a boil. Reduce heat to low, cover and simmer for 5 minutes. Add orzo and simmer for 5 more minutes. Add chicken and simmer for 5 more minutes. Remove from heat and stir in parsley. Serve hot.

Makes about 8 cups soup

Per cup: 141 calories, 4.4 g total fat (1 g saturated fat), 10.7 g protein, 15.4 g carbohydrate (1.5 g fiber, 3.4 g sugars), 29 mg cholesterol, 263 mg sodium

Since it's tasty and convenient, I like using equal amounts of light meat and dark meat from a rotisserie chicken in this recipe. Plus, this shortcut helps speed up the cooking process, which means I'm devouring tasty soup in under 30 minutes. Wanna make it the old-fashion way? Here's how: Buy 6 large, bone-in, skin-on chicken thighs. Remove the skin, keep the bones. Bones are good in soup making! Heat the olive oil in the soup over medium-high heat and brown the chicken thighs on both sides. Remove them from the pot and set them aside for now. Add a bit more oil to the pot, then proceed with the recipe as written, adding the chicken thighs back to the pot when you add the broth. Simmer for 20 minutes, THEN add the orzo and simmer until it's tender. Orzo usually takes about 8 minutes to cook, max. Carefully remove the cooked chicken thighs from the pot, let them cool a bit, then cut the meat off the bones and return the meat to the pot. Stir in parsley and serve.

SCAN FOR VIDEO!

Feel-good soup

YUM
Throw in a small handful of baby spinach when you add the chicken.

YUMMER!
Top individual servings with freshly grated Parmesan cheese.

Silky Roasted Butternut Squash Soup
with Apples & Sage

Silky, creamy, sweet and savory, roasting the squash makes it super flavory!

Alright, so I'll never win any poetry awards. I get that. Regardless, there's no rhyme or reason why you shouldn't make this simple squash soup. It's company-worthy, spoon-worthy, swoon-worthy! And in case you were wondering, the white beans add substance and fiber, but don't change the taste. And when you eat more fiber, you can whittle your waist. See what I did there?

1 large or 2 small butternut squash, about 3 lbs (1.4 kg) total

2 tsp olive oil

1 tbsp butter (or olive oil for vegan)

1½ cups chopped sweet onions

1 large sweet apple, peeled and coarsely chopped

1 tbsp minced fresh sage

¼ tsp each ground cinnamon and ground ginger

4 cups reduced-sodium vegetable broth

1 cup cooked navy beans or white kidney beans

½ tsp each sea salt and freshly ground black pepper

⅓ cup half-and-half (10%) cream (optional but really nice; omit for vegan)

Note: Roasting the squash MAKES this recipe, as I stated in my "poem" above. If you don't feel like roasting squash, make a new dinner plan, Stan. I'm serious!

Preheat oven to 425°F. Line a rimmed baking sheet with foil or parchment paper and set aside.

Using a large, sharp knife and a sense of caution, carefully slice the squash in half lengthwise. Count your fingers. Still 10? Good. You may proceed! Scoop out and discard the seeds.

Brush the cut sides of squash with olive oil. Place squash cut-side up on prepared baking sheet. Roast for 45 minutes, or until squash is tender and lightly browned and slightly caramelized. Yum! Remove from oven and let squash cool for a bit.

Melt butter in a large soup pot over medium heat. Add onions and apples. Cook slowly, stirring often, until onions and apples are softened, about 5 minutes. Don't rush it. Stir in sage, cinnamon and ginger. Mix well. Add broth, beans, salt and pepper.

Scoop out the flesh from the roasted squash and add it to the pot. Bring soup to a boil. Reduce heat to low and simmer, covered, for 15 minutes. Using an immersion blender, purée soup until perfectly smooth. Stir in cream, if using. Serve hot.

Make about 7 cups soup

Per cup: 149 calories, 4.6 g total fat (2 g saturated fat), 3.5 g protein, 25 g carbohydrate (3.6 g fiber, 6.8 g sugars), 9 mg cholesterol, 259 mg sodium

SCAN FOR VIDEO!

YUM
A large, ripe pear would work well in place of the apple.

YUMMER!
Company coming? Go all out and upgrade the half-and-half to heavy (whipping) cream.

THE BOWLED AND THE BEAUTIFUL

Mexican Lentil Soup

I fell in love with Mexican Lentil Soup the second I tried it at a new vegetarian restaurant in my neighborhood. It's similar to chili, but not as heavy, with just the right amount of spice. The slight hint of cinnamon tastes *cin*sational! Plus, lentils are PACKED with protein and fiber, so they really fill you up. It's basically a bowlful of goodness and one of my favorite vegan soups.

1 tbsp olive oil

1 cup each diced onions, diced celery and diced red bell peppers

1 tsp minced garlic

1 cup peeled, cubed sweet potatoes (small cubes)

2 tsp each chili powder and ground cumin

1 tsp each ground coriander and dried oregano

½ tsp ground cinnamon

3 cups reduced-sodium vegetable broth

1 can (14 oz/398 mL) fire-roasted diced tomatoes (with liquid)

3 tbsp smoky barbecue sauce (store-bought or homemade)**

½ tsp each sea salt and freshly ground black pepper

1 can (19 oz/540 mL) lentils, drained and rinsed

2 to 3 tbsp minced fresh cilantro

Diced avocados (for vegan) and/or Greek yogurt or sour cream for topping, optional

* This soup is dairy-free and vegan. The optional Greek yogurt/sour cream topping is not.

** Make sure your barbecue sauce is gluten-free and/or vegan if that's important to you. There are lots of options on store shelves, so this shouldn't be a problem.

Heat olive oil in a large soup pot over medium heat. Add onions, celery, bell peppers and garlic. Cook and stir until vegetables begin to soften, about 5 minutes.

Add sweet potatoes, chili powder, cumin, coriander, oregano and cinnamon. Mix well. Add broth, tomatoes with their liquid, barbecue sauce, salt and pepper. Bring soup to a boil. Reduce heat to low, cover and simmer for 20 minutes. Stir in lentils and simmer for 5 more minutes.

Remove soup from heat. Using an immersion blender, purée about half the soup using quick pulses, so it's still a bit lumpy but appears thicker (see photo). Stir in cilantro. Serve with diced avocados or Greek yogurt/sour cream dollop (for non-vegan).

Makes about 7 cups soup

Per cup: 162 calories, 2.9 g total fat (0.4 g saturated fat), 7.3 g protein, 27.5 g carbohydrate (8.4 g fiber, 6 g sugars), 0 mg cholesterol, 468 mg sodium

SCAN FOR VIDEO!

HEALTHY
HEARTY
Heavenly

YUM
Try using carrots or
butternut squash
instead of sweet potatoes.

YUMMER!
Top with grated cheddar or Monterey
Jack cheese before serving.

Thai Green Curry Superfood Soup
with Kale, Broccoli & Coconut Milk

I love Thai green curry ANYTHING. You could simmer dog kibble in Thai green curry sauce and I'd happily eat it. Last time I ordered Thai green curry chicken at a restaurant, I used a spoon to slurp up every last drop of the outrageously delicious sauce. That's when it dawned on me that a green curry soup would be easy to make and taste totally Thai-rific.

1 tbsp coconut oil or olive oil

1 cup chopped onions

3 tbsp Thai green curry paste

1 tbsp grated fresh gingerroot

1 tsp minced garlic

3 cups reduced-sodium vegetable broth

1 can (14 oz/398 mL) coconut milk (light or regular)

4 cups coarsely chopped broccoli florets

1 tbsp fish sauce or reduced-sodium soy sauce
(use Tamari soy sauce for gluten-free)

1 tbsp freshly squeezed lime juice

½ tsp grated lime zest

3 cups packed chopped kale (ribs removed)

1 cup frozen green peas, thawed

¼ cup each chopped fresh cilantro and
chopped fresh basil

* For vegan soup, use soy sauce instead of fish sauce.

Heat coconut oil in a large soup pot over medium heat. Add onions. Cook until onions begin to soften, about 3 minutes. Add curry paste, gingerroot and garlic. Cook 1 more minute. Add broth, coconut milk, broccoli, fish sauce, lime juice and zest. Bring soup to a boil. Reduce heat to low, cover and simmer for 6 minutes. Add kale and peas, mix well and simmer for 5 more minutes. Stir in cilantro and basil. Remove soup from heat.

Working in batches, CAREFULLY transfer soup to a blender and purée until perfectly smooth. I like to work in three small batches. Serve hot.

Makes about 8 cups soup

Per cup: 143 calories, 9.2 g total fat (7.8 g saturated fat), 3.2 g protein, 11.7 g carbohydrate (2.4 g fiber, 4 g sugars), 0 mg cholesterol, 375 mg sodium

Since I love making soup, an immersion (handheld) blender is one of my favorite cooking tools. However, if you want the silkiest, creamiest, dreamiest soup texture, you'll get better results using a high-powered blender. To avoid a major blender blunder (a.k.a hot soup explosion) follow these tips: (1) Never fill the blender more than half full with soup. One-third full is even better; (2) Remove the center piece of the blender lid; (3) Place lid securely on blender; (4) Cover the hole with a folded dishcloth and hold lid down; (5) Begin blending at the lowest speed and slowly increase the speed as needed. Note: Some high-end blenders like Vitamix and Blendtec have a special lid that vents steam pressure without needing to remove the center part. You still need to be careful though!

SCAN FOR VIDEO!

Superfoods: broccoli, kale, gingerroot, garlic

Nourishing
Bone Broth

GF **DF**

Bone broth is a hot health-food trend, but it's not a fad. It's been around FOREVER and has a history dating back to prehistoric times. Thankfully, it's very easy to make at home. I love sipping on a mug of bone broth instead of coffee in the morning or enjoying a cup before bed. I made and drank bone broth regularly when recovering from knee surgery. I'm a totally unscientific study of one—but I truly believe that the healing properties of bone broth helped me shift from chronically limping in pain to joyfully running up flights of stairs. I suppose my orthopedic surgeon had something to do with it, too. ☺

3 lbs (1.4 kg) beef bones*

1 medium onion, quartered

3 small carrots, scrubbed, cut in half

2 large celery stalks, cut in half

3 bay leaves

3 or 4 sprigs fresh thyme

2 tsp sea salt

2 tsp whole black peppercorns

16 cups pure filtered water

2 tbsp raw apple cider vinegar
(helps extract the minerals and other good stuff from the bones)

* For the bones, I use a combination of marrow bones and beef feet. Sounds awful, I know! But it's the knuckly, jointy parts that create the gelatin, which has the beneficial collagen. Make sure the bones aren't huge. About 3 inches max. A butcher can cut them for you. Try your best to use high-quality bones from organic, pasture-raised beef.

Place beef bones on a rimmed baking sheet and roast them, uncovered, for 30 minutes at 375°F. This makes them taste better. A bunch of fat will likely pool on the tray…throw it out.

Put roasted bones and all remaining ingredients in your largest soup pot (you need a BIG one!) and bring to a boil. Reduce heat AS LOW AS POSSIBLE without shutting off your stove. Broth should be simmering very gently, not boiling. Cover with lid (make sure your lid doesn't have a steam hole) and simmer for 24 hours.

Let broth cool slightly, then strain it using a fine mesh sieve so it's clear. Discard the bones, herbs and cooked vegetables. Taste and add more salt and pepper if needed. Cool broth on stovetop. When cool enough to refrigerate, store it in the fridge. When it's cold, it'll have a layer of fat on top. Skim this off and throw it out. The broth should have a wiggly, jelly-like consistency. Scoop up the amount you need and heat it. Bone broth will keep for a week in the fridge or you can easily freeze it. Sip, sip hooray!

Makes about 14 cups broth

Per cup**: 50 calories, 3 g total fat (0.5 g saturated fat), 7 g protein, 1 g carbohydrate (0 g fiber, 0 g sugars), 10 mg cholesterol, 330 mg sodium

** This is an estimate. Without an expensive lab analysis, it's almost impossible to determine the exact nutrition numbers for bone broth.

SCAN FOR VIDEO!

The TOP 5 Benefits of Bone Broth

1. Helps reduce joint pain and inflammation.
2. Helps repair leaky gut syndrome.
3. Helps your skin glow and your hair grow!
4. Helps strengthen your immune system.
5. Helps improve sleep and brain function.

To bone up on broth benefits, I highly recommend the book *Nourishing Broth: An Old-Fashioned Remedy for a Modern World* by Sally Fallon Morell.

Nutritious & HEALTH-BOOSTING

Sweet Potato & Black Bean Chili
with Kale

Throw this beautiful, colorful, veggie-and-bean-packed chili into your Meatless Monday rotation! It's so tasty and satisfying, no one will miss the meat (but you could definitely add some if you want). Don't be intimidated by the long list of ingredients…they're all very common and many will already be in your kitchen!

1 tbsp olive oil

1½ cups chopped onions

1½ cups chopped green bell peppers

1 jalapeño pepper, minced

2 tsp minced garlic

3 cups peeled, cubed sweet potatoes

4 tsp chili powder

2 tsp ground cumin

1 tsp dried oregano

½ tsp smoked paprika*

¼ tsp cayenne pepper (optional)

1 can (28 oz/798 mL) no-salt-added diced tomatoes (with liquid)

2 cups reduced-sodium vegetable broth

1 can (14 oz/398 mL) no-salt-added tomato sauce

½ tsp each sea salt and freshly ground black pepper

2 cans (19 oz/540 mL each) no-salt-added black beans, drained and rinsed

2 cups packed chopped kale (ribs removed)

3 tbsp minced fresh cilantro

1 tbsp freshly squeezed lime juice

* The smoked paprika makes the chili taste a little, well, smoky! If you don't have it, you can use regular paprika. This chili's a bit spicy, so if heat's not your thing, omit the jalapeño and the cayenne pepper.

Heat olive oil in a large soup pot over medium-high heat. Add onions, bell peppers, jalapeño and garlic. Cook and stir until vegetables begin to soften, about 5 minutes. Be careful not to burn the garlic (reduce heat if necessary).

Add sweet potatoes, chili powder, cumin, oregano, paprika and cayenne, if using. Mix well, until potatoes are coated with seasoning. Add tomatoes with their liquid, broth, tomato sauce, salt and pepper. Mix well. Bring mixture to a boil. Reduce heat to low, cover and simmer for 15 minutes.

Stir in beans and kale. Simmer for 10 more minutes, or until sweet potatoes are tender. Remove from heat and stir in cilantro and lime juice. Serve hot.

Makes about 8 cups chili

Per cup: 264 calories, 3.6 g total fat (0.3 g saturated fat), 12 g protein, 48 g carbohydrate (13 g fiber, 10.4 g sugars), 0 mg cholesterol, 306 mg sodium

 SCAN FOR VIDEO!

A GREAT *source of* *vegan protein:* 12 GRAMS PER CUP!

YUM
Use one can black beans + one can chickpeas.

YUMMER!
Top the chili with diced avocados right before serving.

Chicken Potpie Chowder

GF

I'd rank homemade chicken potpie as one of my all-time favorite splurge-worthy comfort foods. I also love chicken soup. So, this creamy, dreamy hybrid is basically potpie filling in soup form. It's one-pot wonderful and a little bit sinful. Time to quit lookin' and start cookin'!

1 tbsp butter

1 cup chopped onions

1 cup diced celery

1 tsp minced garlic

2½ cups reduced-sodium chicken broth*

2 cups peeled, cubed potatoes

1½ tsp dried thyme

½ tsp poultry seasoning

½ tsp sea salt

¼ tsp freshly ground black pepper

1 can (14 oz/398 mL) cream-style corn

1 cup frozen peas and carrots

2 cups chopped cooked chicken breast

1 cup half-and-half (10%) cream**

1 tbsp cornstarch

1 to 2 tbsp minced fresh parsley

* If it's important to you that the recipe is gluten-free, make sure you use gluten-free chicken broth.

** To lighten up the recipe, use 2% evaporated milk instead of cream. The soup will still be delicious, I promise!

In a large soup pot, melt butter over medium heat. Add onions, celery and garlic. Cook and stir until vegetables begin to soften, about 3 minutes.

Add broth, potatoes, thyme, poultry seasoning, salt and pepper. Bring to a boil, then reduce heat to low and simmer, covered, for 10 minutes. Add cream-style corn and peas and carrots. Simmer for 5 more minutes. Stir in chopped chicken and mix well.

In a measuring cup, whisk together cream and cornstarch until smooth with no lumps. Add to chicken mixture in pot. Increase heat so the chowder comes to a gentle simmer and begins to thicken. Stir often. Add parsley and serve hot.

Makes about 10 cups chowder

Per cup: 148 calories, 5.1 g total fat (2.7 g saturated fat), 9.5 g protein, 17 g carbohydrate (2 g fiber, 3.8 g sugars), 32 mg cholesterol, 196 mg sodium

SCAN FOR VIDEO!

WHOLE WHEAT
pumpkin biscuits
PAGE 250

Wickedly Delicious
SPLURGE-WORTHY
Totally Worth It!

YUM
Instead of cooked chicken,
use up your leftover turkey!

YUMMER!
Serve with buttery, homemade
biscuits for dunking.

Slow Cooker Chicken, Veggie & Brown Rice Soup

Throw everything in your slow cooker and forget about it until dinnertime. What's not to love about that? This recipe makes a BIG pot of hearty, healthy soup that appeals to all ages and taste buds. Freeze the leftovers!

1 tbsp olive oil

6 large bone-in chicken thighs, skin removed (about 1½ lbs/680 g)

1½ cups each diced celery, diced carrots and diced onions

1 can (28 oz/798 mL) no-salt-added diced tomatoes (with liquid)

4 cups reduced-sodium chicken broth

4 cups garden vegetable cocktail (see Kitchen Whizdom)

½ cup uncooked brown rice (or pearl barley)

1 tsp each dried thyme, dried marjoram and dried sage

½ tsp each sea salt and freshly ground black pepper

Heat olive oil in a large skillet over medium-high heat. Add chicken thighs and cook until browned on both sides (but not cooked through). Transfer chicken thighs to a 6-qt or larger slow cooker.

Add all remaining ingredients and mix well. Cover and cook on low setting for 8 hours or high setting for 5 hours.

Carefully remove chicken thighs to a cutting board and let cool slightly. Cut meat off the bones into bite-sized pieces and return to crock. Mix well. Taste and add more salt and pepper if needed. Enjoy!

Makes about 12 cups soup

Per cup: 146 calories, 3.4 g total fat (0.7 g saturated fat), 12 g protein, 17 g carbohydrate (3.2 g fiber, 6 g sugars), 39 mg cholesterol, 455 mg sodium

Try Mott's Garden Cocktail or V8 juice in this recipe. Both products are available in reduced-sodium varieties. Yeah, it's a bit of a pain to cut the meat off the chicken bones after cooking, but using bones in soup makes it taste better. My Polish mother, Alfreda, says so—and she's always been a fabulous soup maker! Like most soups, this one tastes even better the next day, once the flavors have had a chance to develop.

SCAN FOR VIDEO!

Freezer Pleaser!

Stuffed Bell Pepper Soup

We all know that guy who says soup's not a meal unless it contains meat, right? I can see you nodding! I guarantee you won't hear any "where's the beef?" complaints when he eats this feast of a soup for dinner, since it's meaty, manly and mighty filling. Plus, it really does taste like a stuffed bell pepper…only much easier to make!

1 tbsp olive oil

1¼ lbs (568 g) extra-lean ground beef

1½ cups diced green bell peppers

1 cup diced onions

2 tsp minced garlic

1½ tsp dried marjoram

1½ tsp chili powder

½ tsp dried basil

½ tsp dried fennel seeds (optional)

4 cups reduced-sodium beef broth

1 can (19 oz/540 mL) petite-cut tomatoes
   (with liquid)

1½ cups tomato sauce
   (see Kitchen Whizdom)

½ tsp freshly ground black pepper

Sea salt to taste

2 cups cooked brown rice

Heat olive oil in a large soup pot over medium-high heat. Add beef. Cook and stir until beef is no longer pink and lightly browned, about 5 minutes. Add bell peppers, onions and garlic. Cook and stir until vegetables begin to soften, about 3 more minutes.

Add marjoram, chili powder, basil and fennel seeds, if using. Cook and stir for 1 more minute. Add beef broth, tomatoes with their liquid, tomato sauce and pepper. Bring soup to a boil. Reduce heat to low and simmer, covered, for 30 minutes. Taste and add salt if needed. (I almost always add salt at this point, depending on the broth I use.)

If serving immediately, stir in cooked rice, then ladle soup into serving bowls. If you're planning on eating the soup over the course of a couple days, keep the rice separate, otherwise it'll soak up all the broth.

Makes about 12 cups soup

Per cup: 174 calories, 6.6 g total fat (2 g saturated fat), 12.7 g protein, 16 g carbohydrate (2.4 g fiber, 4.6 g sugars), 26 mg cholesterol, 222 mg sodium

I don't like big pieces of vegetables in this soup, so I dice the onions and bell peppers small and use "petite-cut" canned tomatoes (usually with green peppers, celery and onions added…a good complement to this soup). You can use plain tomato sauce or your favorite, tomato-based pasta sauce for extra flavor. For example, I often use Classico brand Sweet Basil Marinara in this soup. By the way, the chili powder doesn't make the soup taste like chili. It just makes it taste BETTER! Use the fennel seeds if you like the mild black-licorice taste of Italian sausage. Those with fennel phobia should leave it out.

SCAN FOR VIDEO!

#soupersatisfying #guyfood

Italian Turkey Sausage, Tomato & White Bean Soup
⇒ with *Kale* ⇐

When winter weather turns wicked, I like to drown my frosty sorrows in this healthy and hearty Italian soup. It not only warms you up, but it's also a good source of protein and fiber, thanks to the turkey sausage, navy beans and nutrient-packed kale.

1 tbsp olive oil

1 lb (454 g) raw Italian turkey sausage, casings removed

1½ cups chopped sweet onions

1 cup each diced carrots and diced celery

2 tsp minced garlic

2 tsp dried Italian seasoning

4 cups reduced-sodium chicken broth

1 can (28 oz/796 mL) no-salt-added diced tomatoes, well drained

¼ cup tomato paste

1 tbsp balsamic vinegar

1 tsp sugar (any kind; I like coconut sugar)

½ tsp each sea salt and freshly ground black pepper

1 bay leaf

1 can (19 oz/540 mL) no-salt-added navy beans, drained and rinsed

3 cups packed chopped fresh kale (ribs removed)

8 fresh basil leaves, chopped

Heat olive oil in a large soup pot over medium-high heat. Add sausage. Cook and stir until sausage is lightly browned, breaking up any large clumps as it cooks. Add onions, carrots, celery and garlic. Cook and stir until vegetables begin to soften, about 5 minutes.

Add Italian seasoning and mix well. Add broth, tomatoes, tomato paste, balsamic vinegar, sugar, salt, pepper and bay leaf. Bring soup to a boil. Reduce heat to low, cover and simmer for 20 minutes.

Add navy beans and kale and simmer for 5 more minutes. Remove soup from heat, remove and discard bay leaf and stir in chopped basil. Taste and add a bit more salt and pepper, if needed. Serve hot.

Makes about 8 cups soup

Per cup: 196 calories, 4.6 g total fat (1 g saturated fat), 14.5 g protein, 26 g carbohydrate (6.2 g fiber, 7.2 g sugars), 0 mg cholesterol, 278 mg sodium

SCAN FOR VIDEO!

YUM
Try baby spinach instead of kale.

YUMMER!
Top with freshly grated (or shaved)
Parmesan cheese before serving (pictured).

SOUP FOR SUPPER!

Roasted Carrot Soup
with Curry & Coconut Milk

Roasting the carrots and onions adds caramelized sweetness to this rich-tasting, warmly spiced soup. Bonus: It's *souper* easy to make, plus it's gluten-free, dairy-free and vegan, so everyone can enjoy it.

2 lbs (907 g) carrots, peeled (or scrubbed) and coarsely chopped (about 4 cups)

1 small sweet potato, peeled and coarsely chopped (about 1½ to 2 cups)

1 medium onion, cut into large chunks

1 clove garlic, peeled, left whole

1 tbsp olive oil or melted coconut oil

6 cups reduced-sodium vegetable broth

2 tsp grated fresh gingerroot

2 tsp curry powder

1 tsp ground cumin

1 tsp ground coriander

½ tsp each freshly ground black pepper and sea salt

1 cup canned coconut milk (light or regular)*

Chopped fresh cilantro for garnish, optional

* Canned coconut milk is very different than the "coconut beverage" sold in cartons beside the almond milk. I consider canned coconut milk to be for cooking and coconut beverage to be for drinking. Coconut beverage is thinner, watered down and has a milder coconut flavor. The canned stuff is much richer and it's what you'll need for this and other recipes.

Preheat oven to 375°F. Place carrots, sweet potatoes, onions and garlic on a rimmed, non-stick baking sheet that's just large enough to hold the veggies in a single layer. Drizzle with oil. Using your hands, mix the vegetables until they're coated with oil. A bit messy, sorry! Roast, uncovered, for about 35 to 40 minutes, until vegetables are tender. Stir once, halfway through cooking time. Be careful not to burn them. Exact roasting time will depend on thickness of vegetables.

Transfer roasted vegetables to a soup pot. Add broth and all spices. Bring to a boil. Reduced heat to low, cover and simmer for 5 minutes.

Remove soup from heat. Add coconut milk. Using an immersion blender, purée soup until perfectly smooth. Alternatively, transfer soup (be careful, it's HOT!) in 3 or 4 small batches to a blender and whirl until smooth. A blender produces a silky, smooth texture, which I prefer…but please don't burn yourself (see Kitchen Whizdom, page 80). Garnish with cilantro, if using. Enjoy!

Makes about 8 cups soup

Per cup: 155 calories, 7.5 g total fat (3.8 g saturated fat), 2 g protein, 20 g carbohydrate (4 g fiber, 8 g sugars), 0 mg cholesterol, 308 mg sodium

SCAN FOR VIDEO!

a little work, A LOT OF FLAVOR

YUM
If you're not a fan of coconut...no worries. Just use 10% cream or even plain Greek yogurt instead. Greek yogurt will make the soup a bit thicker.

YUMMER!
Add a pretty swirl of coconut milk or cream before serving. See video for how-to. It's EASY!

Turkey, Pumpkin & White Bean Chili

GF **DF**

Your family will gobble up this high-fiber, high-flavor ground turkey and white bean chili! And no one will detect the pumpkin flavor—I promise. The pumpkin simply adds a nutritious hit of beta-carotene and vitamin A, plus it gives the broth a rich, velvety texture.

1 tbsp olive oil

1½ lbs (680 g) lean ground turkey

1½ cups chopped onions

2 tsp minced garlic

1 cup chopped green bell peppers

¾ cup each diced celery and diced carrots

1½ tbsp chili powder

2 tsp ground cumin

1 tsp dried oregano

⅛ tsp cayenne pepper (optional)

2 cups reduced-sodium chicken broth

1 can (19 oz/540 mL) no-salt-added diced tomatoes (with liquid)

1½ cups canned pure pumpkin (not pumpkin pie filling)

1 can (19 oz/540 mL) no-salt-added navy beans, drained and rinsed

2 tbsp minced fresh cilantro

1 tbsp freshly squeezed lime juice

Heat olive oil in a large soup pot over medium-high heat. Add turkey, onions and garlic. Cook and stir until turkey is no longer pink and onions begin to soften, about 5 minutes. Break up any large pieces of turkey as it's cooking.

Add green peppers, celery, carrots, chili powder, cumin, oregano and cayenne pepper, if using. Cook for 1 more minute. Add chicken broth, tomatoes with their liquid and pumpkin. Mix well. Bring mixture to a boil. Reduce heat to low, cover and simmer for 20 minutes.

Stir in beans and simmer for 10 more minutes. Remove from heat. Stir in cilantro and lime juice. Serve hot.

Makes about 10 cups chili

Per cup: 217 calories, 6.8 g total fat (1.9 g saturated fat), 18 g protein, 21 g carbohydrate (6.7 g fiber, 5.2 g sugars), 50 mg cholesterol, 235 mg sodium

KITCHEN WHIZDOM

Can the can? Why not, when it's so easy to cook inexpensive dried beans? Just rinse the dried beans with cold water, then put them in a pot and cover with water, about two inches higher than the beans. Let 'em soak overnight. They'll expand. Drain. Return beans to the pot, cover with water again and simmer about 45 minutes or so until tender. Exact cooking time varies by bean type. I drain and rinse them again in cold water to stop the cooking process, then freeze the beans in 2-cup baggies. This way, I always have cooked beans ready to go, with no salt added, no brine to rinse off and no weird chemicals lining the can's interior. That being said, canned beans are so "can"venient, aren't they? I alternate between cooking beans myself and buying canned beans, which I always drain and rinse well before using.

SCAN FOR VIDEO!

Pumpkin in the broth makes it *VELVETY SMOOTH & super scrumptious!*

YUM
Ground chicken works equally well in this recipe.

YUMMER!
Top chili with sliced avocados and/or sour cream.

CHAPTER 4

Meatless
&
MARVELOUS

Livin' on the vedge is easy
when meals taste this good!

YUM & YUMMER

Beets & Sweets Buddha Bowls
with Creamy Balsamic Dressing

Sometimes called a Hippie Bowl or a Glory Bowl, a Buddha Bowl is basically just a giant bowl filled with hearty, nutritious, vibrantly colored yumminess. Roasted veggies, kale and quinoa topped with creamy balsamic dressing make this blissful bowl a thing of beauty!

Creamy Balsamic Dressing

¼ cup olive oil

2 tbsp white balsamic vinegar

2 tbsp mayonnaise

1 tbsp freshly squeezed lemon juice

2 tsp pure maple syrup or liquid honey

1 tsp Dijon mustard

½ tsp minced garlic

¼ tsp each sea salt and freshly ground
black pepper

2 cups peeled, cubed beets (½-inch cubes)

3 tsp olive oil, divided

2 cups peeled, cubed sweet potatoes
(½-inch cubes)

1 small red onion, cut into wedges

2 cups coarsely chopped kale
(ribs removed)

¼ cup walnut pieces

2 cups hot cooked quinoa or brown rice

¼ cup crumbled light or regular feta
cheese (1 oz/28 g)

Whisk together all dressing ingredients in a small bowl or measuring cup. Cover and refrigerate until ready to use. Line a medium baking pan with parchment paper and preheat oven to 425°F.

In a medium bowl, toss beets with 1 tsp oil. Spread on prepared pan and roast for 15 minutes. Remove beets from oven and move them to one side of the pan.

Toss sweet potatoes and onions with 1 tsp oil and add to beets in a single layer on pan. Roast for 15 minutes. Remove pan from oven and slide the potatoes and onions over next to the beets. Toss kale with remaining 1 tsp oil (massage it in!) and add to veggies in a single layer on pan, then add walnut pieces. (You won't coat the walnuts in oil.) Roast for 5 more minutes.

To assemble, place 1 cup quinoa in bottom of serving bowl. Top with veggies, walnuts and feta, then drizzle dressing over top. Serve warm.

Makes 2 servings

Per serving (without dressing): 540 calories, 17 g total fat (3.2 g saturated fat), 16 g protein, 85 g carbohydrate (13 g fiber, 16 g sugars), 4 mg cholesterol, 379 mg sodium

Dressing per serving (1 tbsp): 66 calories, 6.6 g total fat (0.9 g saturated fat), 0 g protein, 2.5 g carbohydrate (0 g fiber, 1.5 g sugars), 1 mg cholesterol, 91 mg sodium

SCAN FOR VIDEO!

YUM
For a vegan option, use vegan mayonnaise and add chickpeas instead of feta cheese.

YUMMER!
Top with a few fresh blueberries. Sounds weird but tastes great!

Bliss in a bowl!

Cauliflower, Chickpea & Sweet Potato Curry
with Kale & Coconut Milk

Hands down my favorite vegan meal! I make a giant vat of this crazy-delicious curry every other week and then practically live on it.

---

1 tbsp coconut oil or olive oil

1 cup chopped onions

2 tsp minced garlic

4 cups small cauliflower florets

3 cups peeled, cubed sweet potatoes

1 tbsp curry powder

1 tbsp grated fresh gingerroot

2 tsp garam masala spice blend

1 tsp ground cumin

1 can (19 oz/540 mL) no-salt-added diced tomatoes (with liquid)

1 can (14 oz/398 mL) coconut milk (light or regular)

1 can (19 oz/540 mL) no-salt-added chickpeas, drained and rinsed

3 cups loosely packed chopped kale (ribs removed)

2 tbsp minced fresh cilantro

Cooked brown rice or quinoa for serving (optional)

Heat coconut oil in a large soup pot over medium heat. Add onions and garlic. Cook and stir until onions begin to soften, about 3 minutes. Add cauliflower and sweet potatoes. Cook and stir for 3 more minutes. Add curry powder, gingerroot, garam masala and cumin. Mix well. Add tomatoes with their liquid and coconut milk. Bring mixture to a boil. Reduce heat to low, cover and simmer for 10 minutes.

Stir in chickpeas and kale. Mix well. Cover and simmer for 5 more minutes, or until cauliflower and sweet potatoes are tender and kale is wilted. Remove from heat. Stir in cilantro and serve hot over cooked rice, if using.

Makes 4 to 6 servings

Per serving (based on 6 servings): 267 calories, 8.7 g total fat (4 g saturated fat), 10 g protein, 39 g carbohydrate (10 g fiber, 10 g sugars), 0 mg cholesterol, 130 mg sodium

Cauliflower is one of the few "white foods" you can feel good about eating because it's loaded with powerful nutrients. It gets lots of love in health articles and blog posts, but not as much love at the dinner table. Why? Well, childhood memories of soggy, overly steamed cauliflower come to mind! My top-3 favorite ways to prepare cauliflower: (1) In curry dishes, like this one!; (2) Tossed with olive oil and herbs, then roasted (see page 220); and (3) Crunchy florets dunked in hummus or a healthy, creamy dip. Raw! Raw! Raw!

SCAN FOR VIDEO!

A
MUST-TRY
recipe!

YUM
Use baby spinach
instead of kale.

YUMMER!
Serve with warm naan bread and/or
a dollop of plain yogurt (non-vegan).

Stuffed Roasted Acorn Squash
✹ with Moroccan-Spiced Quinoa ✹

Overflowing (literally!) with a Moroccan-spiced quinoa filling, this posh roasted squash makes a stunning, vegan main course or a spectacular side dish at any festive gathering.

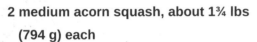

2 medium acorn squash, about 1¾ lbs
 (794 g) each

1 tbsp melted butter or vegan buttery spread*

2 tsp pure maple syrup

¼ tsp ground cinnamon

1¾ cups reduced-sodium vegetable broth

1 cup uncooked quinoa**

¼ cup dried currants

1 tsp ground cumin

1 tsp curry powder

½ tsp ground coriander

¼ tsp sea salt

2 cups baby spinach, coarsely chopped

¼ cup sliced almonds

2 tbsp minced fresh parsley, cilantro or mint

* If serving vegan friends, be sure to use vegan buttery spread instead of butter.

** A combination of red and white quinoa looks nice!

Preheat oven to 400°F. Wash squash, pat dry and slice in half crosswise. Scoop out and discard seeds. Place squash cut-side up on a large baking sheet.

In a small bowl, whisk together butter, maple syrup and cinnamon. Brush over cut sides of squash and inside empty cavity. Roast squash, uncovered, for 1 hour or until caramelized and very tender.

Meanwhile, make filling. In a medium pot, bring broth and quinoa to a boil over medium-high heat. Reduce heat to low, stir in currants, cumin, curry, coriander and salt. Cover and simmer for 12 to 15 minutes, or until liquid is absorbed and quinoa is cooked. Remove from heat, stir in spinach, cover and let stand for 10 minutes or until squash is ready.

When squash is done, stir almonds and parsley into quinoa mixture. Stuff quinoa mixture into empty squash cavities until overflowing. Serve immediately.

Makes 4 servings

Per serving: 322 calories, 8.2 g total fat (2 g saturated fat), 9 g protein, 58 g carbohydrate (7.7 g fiber, 11 g sugars), 8 mg cholesterol, 254 mg sodium

 SCAN FOR VIDEO!

Stuff it!

YUM
Try garam masala spice blend instead of cinnamon.

YUMMER!
Use small, bulbous butternut squash instead of acorn squash. Big bulb = more room for stuffing!

Speedy Chana Masala
a.k.a. Savory Indian Chickpeas

GF DF V

Featuring a healthy, highly seasoned mixture of protein-and-fiber-rich chickpeas, caramelized onions and zesty tomatoes simmered in warm Indian spices, chana masala is a simple yet satisfying plant-based meal.

1 tbsp coconut oil or olive oil

1½ cups chopped onions

1 tbsp minced fresh gingerroot

2 tsp minced garlic

1 tsp curry powder

1 tsp garam masala spice blend

1 tsp ground cumin

½ tsp each ground coriander and
   chili powder

1 can (28 oz/798 mL) no-salt-added diced
   tomatoes (with liquid)

1 can (19 oz/540 mL) no-salt-added
   chickpeas, drained and rinsed

3 tbsp minced fresh cilantro

Sea salt to taste

Heat coconut oil in a medium, non-stick pot over medium heat. Add onions. Cook and stir until onions are very tender and begin to caramelize, about 5 minutes. Don't rush and don't burn them!

Add gingerroot, garlic, curry powder, garam masala, cumin, coriander and chili powder. Cook and stir for 30 seconds. Add tomatoes with their liquid. Bring mixture to a boil. Reduce heat to low, cover and simmer for 10 minutes.

Stir in chickpeas and simmer for 5 more minutes. Remove from heat and add cilantro and salt to taste. Serve hot over cooked brown rice, quinoa or your favorite grain.

Makes 4 meal-sized servings or 6 side-dish servings

Per serving (based on 4 servings): 225 calories, 5.6 g total fat (0.8 g saturated fat), 9 g protein, 36 g carbohydrate (8.8 g fiber, 9.5 g sugars), 0 mg cholesterol, 93 mg sodium

The "chana" part of chana masala refers to the type of chickpea traditionally used in this super-popular Indian dish. The "masala" part refers to the warm spice blend. I'm a big fan of all those warm "C" spices—cumin, curry, coriander, chili powder, cinnamon, cardamom, cayenne, cloves—and I add them to tons of recipes, just in case you haven't noticed. Plus, using mostly "C" spices makes alphabetically organizing my spice rack much easier. LOL!

SCAN FOR VIDEO!

CHICKPEAS?
Yes, please!

YUM
Serve with warm
naan bread to soak
up the sauce.

YUMMER!
I LOVE adding ½ cup coconut milk and a
handful of baby spinach to this recipe.
Stir them in when you add the chickpeas.

Five Ps in a Pot
~ Pasta, Peas, Parmesan, Parsley, Pepper ~

GF

Have you ever stared blankly into your pantry or fridge, only to realize there's absolutely nothing to eat? This recipe, a surprising hit on my Facebook page, is a result of my blank stares mixed with one part desperation and two parts growling stomach. Pasta, peas, Parmesan, parsley and pepper. Perfect! (Though not a "P," the lemon is key. Don't skip it.)

12 oz (340 g) uncooked quinoa spaghetti
  (or whole-grain spaghetti; see Kitchen Whizdom)
1 cup frozen green peas, thawed
3 tbsp butter
2 tbsp freshly squeezed lemon juice
½ cup freshly grated Parmesan cheese
2 tbsp minced fresh parsley
1 tsp grated lemon zest
Freshly ground black pepper to taste

Cook pasta according to package directions, adding the peas during the last 3 minutes of cooking time. Drain pasta and peas in a colander and return the empty, hot pot to stovetop.

Add butter and lemon juice to pot and stir until butter is melted. Return pasta and peas to pot and toss using tongs until pasta is coated with lemon-butter. Add Parmesan, parsley, lemon zest and pepper and toss again. Serve immediately.

Makes 4 servings

Per serving: 464 calories, 13 g total fat (8 g saturated fat), 12.5 g protein, 75 g carbohydrate (8 g fiber, 4 g sugars), 33 mg cholesterol, 263 mg sodium

If you can't find quinoa spaghetti but want a gluten-free option, try brown-rice spaghetti, which is widely available. The key to successfully cooking gluten-free pasta is using TONS of water. Way more than you'd typically use. That's because gluten-free pasta is usually starchier than regular pasta. This extra starch also produces lots of foam, which can easily boil over and create a frothy mess on your stovetop. I use an extra-large pot and fill it two-thirds full of water when cooking a package of pasta. Stir the pasta often, especially at the beginning, so it doesn't stick together. Finally, gluten-free pasta is dreadfully dull without salt, so be generous when salting the cooking water.

SCAN FOR VIDEO!

Wickedly Delicious
SPLURGE-WORTHY
Totally Worth It!

YUM
Try this simple recipe with plump rotini noodles instead of spaghetti.

YUMMER!
For a non-vegetarian meal, toss in some drained, canned tuna (in olive oil) or chopped, leftover salmon when adding the Parmesan and parsley.

Busy Weeknight Lasagna Roll-Ups
with Spinach, Pumpkin & Ricotta Filling

A fun way to eat lasagna, this super-easy dinner idea gets a double thumbs-up from everyone who tastes it. Sneaking pumpkin into the filling makes it more nutritious and, best of all, kids WON'T be suspicious! Tip: Prepare the filling one day in advance to make meal prep easier.

2 cups part-skim ricotta cheese

1 pkg (10 oz/280 g) frozen chopped spinach, thawed and squeezed dry

½ cup freshly grated Parmesan cheese

½ cup canned pure pumpkin (not pumpkin pie filling)

1 egg

¼ tsp each sea salt and freshly ground black pepper

Pinch nutmeg

12 whole wheat lasagna noodles

1 jar (25 oz/700 mL) marinara sauce

½ cup shredded part-skim mozzarella cheese (2 oz/57 g)

To make filling, combine ricotta, spinach, Parmesan, pumpkin, egg, salt, pepper and nutmeg in a medium bowl. Mix well. Cover and refrigerate until ready to use.

Preheat oven to 375°F. Spray a 9 x 13-inch casserole dish with cooking spray or lightly oil. Cook lasagna noodles according to package directions, but slightly undercook them (so they don't rip when rolling). Drain and rinse with cold water.

Spread ¾ cup marinara sauce over bottom of casserole dish. To assemble roll-ups, evenly spread ¼ to ⅓ cup filling over one side of each cooked noodle. Spoon a tablespoon or so of marinara sauce down the center over filling. Roll up and place seam-side down* in casserole dish. Top with remaining marinara sauce and sprinkle with mozzarella. Cover loosely with foil and bake for 25 minutes. Uncover and bake for 10 more minutes. Serve hot.

* In the photo, my roll-ups are standing up so I could show off the fabulous filling.

Makes 12 roll-ups

Per roll-up: 195 calories, 6.2 g total fat (3.3 g saturated fat), 12.4 g protein, 22 g carbohydrate (4.1 g fiber, 4 g sugars), 38 mg cholesterol, 292 mg sodium

SCAN FOR VIDEO!

GET READY
to roll!

YUM
Try cooked, mashed sweet potatoes instead of pumpkin.

YUMMER!
Make roll-ups using the roasted squash filling and creamy Alfredo sauce on page 216 for a decadent addition to your holiday menu.

Thick & Hearty
Lentil & Mushroom Pasta Sauce

My easy-to-make version of meatless Bolognese (an oxymoron, I know!) uses lentils
and mushrooms to create a satisfying vegan sauce for any type of pasta.
Make a double batch and keep some in the freezer!

Meatless

1 tbsp olive oil

1 cup diced onions

⅔ cup each diced carrots and diced celery

2 tsp minced garlic

3 cups finely chopped mushrooms*

1 jar (25 oz/700 mL) marinara sauce
(see Kitchen Whizdom)

1 can (19 oz/540 mL) petite-cut tomatoes
(with liquid)

1 tbsp balsamic vinegar or a splash
of red wine

2 tsp dried Italian seasoning or 1 tsp
each dried oregano and dried basil

1 can (19 oz/540 mL) lentils, drained
and rinsed

2 tbsp minced fresh parsley (optional)

* Finely chop one 8-oz (227 g) package of
mushrooms to get 3 cups. I like cremini or
baby bellas for this recipe.

Heat olive oil in a large soup pot over medium-high heat.
Add onions, carrots, celery and garlic. Cook and stir until
vegetables begin to soften, about 3 minutes. Add mushrooms
and continue to cook until mushrooms are tender, about
5 minutes.

Stir in marinara sauce, tomatoes with their liquid, vinegar
and Italian seasoning. Bring mixture to a boil. Reduce heat
to low, cover and simmer for 15 minutes. Add lentils and
cook for 5 more minutes. Remove from heat and stir in
parsley, if using. Serve over hot pasta.

Makes about 8 cups sauce

Per cup: 156 calories, 2.8 g total fat (0.3 g saturated fat), 7.7 g protein,
26 g carbohydrate (7.6 g fiber, 7.5 g sugars), 0 mg cholesterol,
335 mg sodium

Choose your favorite tomato-based pasta sauce (marinara) to use in this recipe. You'll need about
3 cups sauce. Check the label for sodium content since it varies dramatically from brand to brand.
If you find the sauce a bit too thick (I love it that way!), add some water or vegetable broth to thin it
out. I must confess, I often eat this sauce without any pasta, straight up in a bowl like a vegetarian
stew. *Stewpendous!*

SCAN FOR
VIDEO!

"BOLOGNESE" with a vegan twist!

YUM
Wanna add more veggies?
Finely dice one small zucchini
and cook it with the mushrooms.

YUMMER!
Tastes great topped with freshly
grated Parmesan cheese (non-vegan).

Sweet Potato Quinoa Cakes
with Black Beans & Cilantro

GF **DF** **V**

These mouthwatering quinoa cakes pack tons of flavor into perfectly portioned patties!
Eat them any time of day as a meal or a snack. (Yup, even for breakfast!)
The roasted red pepper hummus is the icing on the cakes. ☺

2 cups peeled, cubed sweet potatoes

2 tsp + 1 tbsp olive oil, divided

1 cup no-salt-added canned black beans, drained and rinsed

1½ cups cooked quinoa, cooled

¼ cup finely minced red onions

3 tbsp minced fresh cilantro

2 tsp minced garlic

2 tsp ground cumin

1 tsp chili powder

½ tsp smoked paprika

¼ tsp each sea salt and freshly ground black pepper

½ cup roasted red pepper hummus (store-bought or homemade; see recipe, page 18)

Preheat oven to 400°F. Line a small baking pan with parchment paper. Spread potato cubes on pan and drizzle with 2 tsp olive oil. Mix well using your hands. Roast potatoes for about 20 minutes, or until tender. Stir once, halfway through cooking time. Transfer to a large bowl, let cool slightly then mash with a fork.

Mash the beans with a fork, leaving them a bit lumpy. Add beans to bowl with potatoes, along with quinoa, onions, cilantro, garlic, cumin, chili powder, paprika, salt and pepper. Mix until all ingredients are well blended. Cover and refrigerate for 1 hour (important).

Form mixture into 3½-inch cakes (using about ½ cup mixture per cake). Heat remaining 1 tbsp olive oil in a 10-inch, non-stick skillet over medium-high heat. Add cakes and cook for about 3 minutes per side, until outside is crispy and inside is heated through. Serve immediately, topped with a dollop of hummus.

Makes 4 to 5 cakes

Per cake (based on 5 cakes): 237 calories, 8.8 g total fat (0.8 g saturated fat), 8 g protein, 33 g carbohydrate (6.7 g fiber, 3 g sugars), 0 mg cholesterol, 267 mg sodium

KITCHEN WHIZDOM

Chilling the quinoa mixture helps the cakes hold their shape when cooking. I've made these cakes many times and they've never fallen apart on me. If you prefer firmer cakes, add 1 lightly beaten egg and ½ cup coarsely ground quick oats to the mixture, then form into 6 patties. Get a head start by cooking the quinoa and the sweet potatoes one day in advance!

 SCAN FOR VIDEO!

MEATLESS
MONDAY
*Dinner
Winner!*

YUM
Try this recipe with
chickpeas instead of
black beans.

YUMMER!
Add ½ cup shredded cheddar
cheese to the quinoa mixture.

ROASTED TOMATO PESTO

1½ lbs (680 g) Roma (plum) tomatoes, quartered
3 tbsp olive oil, divided
Sea salt and freshly ground black pepper
4 cloves garlic
1 cup packed fresh basil
⅓ cup freshly grated Parmesan cheese
¼ cup toasted pine nuts

Line a baking sheet with parchment paper and spread tomatoes in a single layer. Drizzle with 1 tbsp olive oil and sprinkle with salt and pepper. Mix using your hands. Wrap the garlic in foil and place on pan with tomatoes. Roast at 400°F for 45 minutes or so, or until super roasty and caramelized. Cool. Add tomatoes and garlic to bowl of food processor along with basil, Parmesan and pine nuts. Whirl while adding remaining 2 tbsp olive oil through feed tube. Makes a super-tasty pizza or pasta sauce!

Makes ¾ cup pesto

GF Classic Basil Pesto

2 cups packed fresh basil
⅓ cup freshly grated Parmesan cheese
(or nutritional yeast for vegan)
¼ cup toasted pine nuts
2 cloves garlic
¼ tsp each sea salt and
freshly ground black pepper
⅓ cup olive oil

To the bowl of a food processor, add basil, Parmesan, pine nuts, garlic, salt and pepper. Get the blades whirling, then stream olive oil through the feed tube and process until smooth, stopping to scrape down sides of bowl if necessary. Take a whiff. Die of bliss.

Toss with pasta or add a spoonful to tomato soup.

Makes ⅔ cup pesto

* Cover and refrigerate pesto for up to 5 days in the fridge. For Nutritional Info, see page 285.

Pesto is the Besto!

SCAN FOR VIDEO!

A mouthful of summer in a sauce!

GF DF V

AVOCADO & SPINACH PESTO

1 cup diced avocados
1 cup packed baby spinach
1 cup packed fresh basil
¼ cup roasted, salted pistachios*
¼ cup nutritional yeast (or Parmesan for non-vegan)
2 tbsp freshly squeezed lemon juice
2 cloves garlic
¼ tsp each sea salt and freshly ground black pepper
¼ cup olive oil

* Use pumpkin seeds for a nut-free version.

To the bowl of a food processor, add avocados, spinach, basil, pistachios, nutritional yeast, lemon juice, garlic, salt and pepper. Get the blades whirling, then stream olive oil through the feed tube and process until smooth, stopping to scrape down sides of bowl if necessary.

Spoon over omelets or frittatas. Use cilantro instead of basil and serve with Mexican dishes.

Makes 1 cup pesto

Peanutty Sesame Noodle Bowl
with Crispy Tofu & Veggies

Combining skinny noodles with creamy peanut sauce makes me ridiculously happy.
And since I'm not a huge tofu fan, this is the only way I'll eat it: Crisped in a pan and combined
with a lip-smacking peanut sauce flavor explosion. Boom!

Peanut Sauce

⅓ cup natural peanut butter

3 tbsp warm water

2 tbsp reduced-sodium soy sauce (use Tamari
  soy sauce for gluten-free)

2 tbsp seasoned rice vinegar

1 tbsp dark sesame oil

2 tsp pure maple syrup (or liquid honey for
  non-vegan)

2 tsp grated fresh gingerroot

2 tsp minced garlic

1 tsp Sriracha hot sauce (optional)

8 oz (227 g) soba noodles (see Kitchen Whizdom)

8 oz (227 g) extra-firm tofu (see Kitchen Whizdom)

2 tsp peanut oil

1 large red bell pepper, very thinly sliced

1 cup frozen green peas, thawed

¾ cup chopped green onions (with white parts)

¼ cup coarsely chopped fresh cilantro

Toasted sesame seeds and/or chopped peanuts
  for garnish (optional)

Whirl together all sauce ingredients in a small blender or food processor until smooth. Set aside until ready to use. Cook noodles according to package directions. Drain, rinse and set aside.

Slice the tofu into ½-inch-thick pieces and blot dry with paper towels. Keep blotting until tofu feels dry to the touch. Cut into cubes.

Heat peanut oil in a deep, 10-inch, non-stick skillet over medium-high heat. Add tofu. Cook for about 2 minutes, or until tofu is lightly browned. Carefully flip pieces to brown opposite sides. Remove tofu from skillet. To same skillet, add bell peppers, peas and onions. Cook and stir until bell peppers are tender, about 3 minutes. Add sauce and heat until bubbly. Turn off heat, then add tofu, noodles and cilantro to skillet. Toss until veggies and noodles are evenly coated with sauce. Garnish with sesame seeds and/or peanuts, if using.

Makes 4 servings

Per serving: 480 calories, 19 g total fat* (2.5 g saturated fat), 20 g protein, 63 g carbohydrate (7.2 g fiber, 11.7 g sugars), 0 mg cholesterol, 389 mg sodium
* You can reduce the fat content by using light peanut butter and 2 tsp sesame oil instead of 1 tbsp.

Can't find soba noodles? No worries. Brown-rice noodles, quinoa spaghetti or whole wheat spaghetti (not gluten-free) would also work. The firmer the tofu, the less water it contains, which is good for stir-frying. However, you still need to press out as much moisture as possible using paper towels, otherwise you'll never get a crispy exterior.

SCAN FOR VIDEO!

NOW THAT'S USING YOUR NOODLE!

YUM
Not a fan of tofu? Use chicken or shrimp!

YUMMER!
Use flavored tofu such as teriyaki or sesame ginger.

Cauli"flour" Crusted Quiche
❧ with Spinach & Mushrooms ❧

Starchy, ordinary pastry crust gets replaced by a flavor-packed, lower-carb (gluten-free!) veggie version in this *eggsquisite* quiche recipe.

Crust

1 small head cauliflower,
  cut into florets
½ cup freshly grated Parmesan cheese
1 egg
½ tsp dried basil
¼ tsp garlic powder
¼ tsp freshly ground black pepper

Filling

2 tsp olive oil
1 cup diced red onions
1 cup diced red bell peppers
2 cups sliced mushrooms
  (I use cremini)
2 cups baby spinach
¾ cup shredded part-skim Swiss or
  Monterey Jack cheese (3 oz/85 g)
5 eggs
⅔ cup 2% evaporated milk or
  5% light cream
1 tsp Dijon mustard
½ tsp dried basil
½ tsp sea salt
¼ tsp freshly ground black pepper

Preheat oven to 350°F. Spray a 9-inch, deep-dish pie plate with cooking spray or brush lightly with oil. Set aside.

In the bowl of a food processor, pulse cauliflower florets until they resemble rice or couscous. (You should end up with about 4 cups "rice.") Spread the cauliflower rice on a small, non-stick baking sheet and bake for 15 minutes. This helps dry out the cauliflower. Remove from oven and let cool. Increase oven temperature to 375°F.

In a large bowl, combine cauliflower, Parmesan, egg, basil, garlic powder and pepper. Mix well. Press mixture over bottom and sides of prepared pie plate. Pat crust with paper towels to remove any excess moisture. Bake for 15 minutes, or until crust is golden.

While crust is baking, prepare filling. Heat olive oil in a 10-inch, non-stick skillet over medium-high heat. Add onions and peppers. Cook and stir until vegetables begin to soften, about 2 minutes. Add mushrooms and cook until mushrooms are tender and start to brown, about 5 minutes. Stir in spinach and cook until wilted. Remove vegetable mixture from heat.

Spoon vegetable mixture evenly over bottom of baked crust. Top with cheese. Whisk together eggs, milk, Dijon, basil, salt and pepper in a large measuring cup. Pour egg mixture over cheese. Bake quiche for about 40 to 45 minutes, or until eggs are set and top is golden. Let cool 5 minutes, then slice and serve.

Makes 6 servings

Per serving: 240 calories, 12.5 g total fat
(4.9 g saturated fat), 18 g protein, 16 g carbohydrate
(4.7 g fiber, 8.7 g sugars), 207 mg cholesterol,
600 mg sodium

SCAN FOR VIDEO!

FLOURLESS &
flavorful!

YUM
Feta cheese is a good
substitute for Swiss
or Monterey Jack.

YUMMER!
For a hearty dinner, serve with
a bowl of your favorite soup.
(Tomato soup would be perfect!)

Mediterranean Grilled Vegetable Pizzas
~ with Multigrain Crusts ~

These loaded, grilled veggie pizzas are the perfect party fare and use pre-fab multigrain crusts to save boatloads of time. Mixing sun-dried tomato pesto with pizza sauce is a flavor trick I've used for years. You've gotta try it!

1 large red bell pepper, chopped

8 oz (227 g) cremini mushrooms, sliced

2 small zucchini, chopped

1 medium red onion, coarsely chopped

1 tbsp olive oil

⅔ cup pizza sauce (store-bought or homemade; see Kitchen Whizdom)

⅓ cup sun-dried tomato pesto

2 10- to 12-inch thin multigrain pizza crusts (store-bought)

⅓ cup sliced or chopped black olives

1 cup shredded part-skim mozzarella cheese (4 oz/113 g)

½ cup crumbled light or regular feta cheese (2 oz/57 g)

2 tbsp minced fresh oregano

Freshly ground black pepper (optional)

Preheat grill to medium-high heat and oven to 425°F.

In a large bowl, toss bell peppers, mushrooms, zucchini and onions with olive oil. Transfer to a grill basket and grill until tender with nice grill marks, stirring often (about 10 to 12 minutes). Cool slightly and chop veggies smaller (so you don't have big chunks on your pizza).

In a small bowl, mix together pizza sauce and pesto. Spread over crusts. Top with veggies, olives, mozzarella and feta.

Bake pizzas in preheated oven directly on middle oven rack for 10 minutes, or until cheese is bubbly and crust is lightly browned. Sprinkle with fresh oregano and top with freshly ground black pepper, if using. Serve immediately.

Makes 2 pizzas, 8 slices each

Per slice: 121 calories, 5.8 g total fat (1.7 g saturated fat), 4.3 g protein, 13.4 g carbohydrate (1.8 g fiber, 2.8 g sugars), 6 mg cholesterol, 259 mg sodium

Want pizza with pizzazz? Make your own sauce! Heat 1 tbsp olive oil in a medium pot over medium heat. Add ½ cup minced red onions and 2 tsp minced garlic. Cook and stir for 3 minutes, until onions are tender. Add 2 cups no-salt-added tomato sauce, 1 small can (5.5 oz/156 mL) tomato paste, 2 tsp dried oregano, 2 tsp balsamic vinegar, 2 tsp brown sugar, ½ tsp each dried basil, dried rosemary and sea salt, plus ¼ tsp freshly ground black pepper. Mix well, bring to a boil, then reduce heat to low, cover and simmer for 15 minutes. Keeps for 1 week in the fridge or 2 months if frozen.

SCAN FOR VIDEO!

YUM
Try pre-shredded
Italian cheese
blend instead of
the mozzarella.

YUMMER!
Serve with tzatziki
sauce (page 150)
for dunking!

A SLICE OF
heaven!

Tex-Mex
Quinoa & Sweet Potato Skillet Meal

GF **DF** **V**

This easy, vegan, one-pot supper with smoky flavors is on the dinner table in about 30 minutes. It's loaded with flavor, fiber and protein, PLUS it makes a tasty taco or burrito filling. *Fabuloso!*

---

1 tbsp olive oil

1 cup chopped onions

2 tsp minced garlic

1 small jalapeño pepper, minced (optional)

2 cups peeled, cubed sweet potatoes

1 tbsp chili powder

2 tsp ground cumin

½ tsp each ground coriander and paprika

¼ tsp cayenne pepper (optional)

1 can (14 oz/398 mL) fire-roasted diced tomatoes (with liquid; see Kitchen Whizdom)

1½ cups reduced-sodium vegetable broth

1 cup uncooked quinoa

1 cup no-salt-added canned black beans, drained and rinsed

1 cup whole-kernel corn (thaw first if using frozen)

2 to 3 tbsp minced fresh cilantro

Sliced avocados and diced tomatoes for garnish (optional)

You will need a deep, 10-inch, non-stick skillet with a lid for this recipe.

Heat olive oil in skillet over medium heat. Add onions, garlic and jalapeño, if using. Cook and stir until onions are tender, about 3 minutes. Add sweet potatoes, chili powder, cumin, coriander, paprika and cayenne, if using. Mix well.

Stir in tomatoes with their liquid, broth and quinoa. Bring mixture to a boil. Reduce heat to low and simmer, covered, for 15 to 20 minutes, until quinoa has absorbed liquid and sweet potatoes are tender.

Stir in beans and corn. Cover and let mixture stand for 10 minutes before serving. This step is important! Stir in cilantro just before serving and garnish with sliced avocados and diced tomatoes, if using.

Makes 4 meal-size servings or 6 side-dish servings

Per serving (based on 4 servings): 367 calories, 7.3 g total fat (0.7 g saturated fat), 12 g protein, 67 g carbohydrate (12 g fiber, 8.8 g sugars), 0 mg cholesterol, 331 mg sodium

Fire-roasted canned tomatoes add a smoky note to this recipe and I highly recommend you try them. They're also super tasty in chili. Muir Glen, Aylmer Accents and Hunt's are three widely available brands of fire-roasted tomatoes. Regular diced tomatoes will work just fine—but I'd suggest using smoked paprika instead of regular paprika to imitate the roasted tomato flavor.

SCAN FOR VIDEO!

YUM
Cook 1 lb (454 g) ground chicken with the onions for a non-vegetarian version.

YUMMER!
Top with your favorite shredded cheese.

12 g plant-based protein
PER SERVING!

CHAPTER 5

Fish DELISH

These savory seafood dishes
are the "reel" deal!

YUM & YUMMER

Roasted Asian Salmon Fillets
with Sesame-Ginger Marinade

GF* DF

Healthy, simple and infused with flavor in every bite, this roasted salmon recipe with sweet and sticky Asian-inspired marinade is one of my favorites! No time to marinate? No problem! Just slather the salmon fillets with the marinade and pop them in the oven.

Marinade

½ cup hoisin sauce*

2 tbsp freshly squeezed lime juice

1 tbsp each liquid honey and reduced-sodium soy sauce*

1 tbsp grated fresh gingerroot (see Kitchen Whizdom)

2 tsp minced garlic

2 tsp dark sesame oil

½ tsp grated lime zest

4 salmon fillets (5 oz/142 g each)
Toasted sesame seeds and slivered green onions for garnish (optional)

* For gluten-free, use GF hoisin sauce and Tamari soy sauce.

In a small bowl or measuring cup, whisk together all marinade ingredients until well blended.

Arrange salmon fillets in a shallow baking dish and pour marinade over top. Turn salmon pieces to coat both sides with marinade. Cover and refrigerate for 2 hours.

Preheat oven to 450°F. Place marinated salmon fillets on a large, rimmed baking sheet lined with parchment paper. Drizzle extra marinade over top. Roast for about 10 minutes, or until salmon is cooked through and flakes easily with a fork. Garnish with sesame seeds and green onions, if using.

Makes 4 servings

Per serving: 289 calories, 12 g total fat (1.9 g saturated fat), 29 g protein, 14.8 g carbohydrate (0.7 g fiber, 10 g sugars), 79 mg cholesterol, 544 mg sodium

If you've cooked from my previous cookbooks, you'd know I'm a HUGE fan of fresh gingerroot. Next to fresh lemons, it's the healthy ingredient I use the most. Open my freezer and you'll always find a little baggy with a big hunk of gingerroot in it. Why the freezer? Cuz gingerroot is so much easier to grate when it's frozen. Peel it, freeze it, grate it! No stringy fibers, no clogged zester, no way you aren't trying this, right?

SCAN FOR VIDEO!

Sticky, gooey, yummy!

YUM
Tastes great served with stir-fried vegetables or steamed broccoli.

YUMMER!
Kick it up a notch by adding ¼ tsp crushed red pepper flakes to the marinade.

15-Minute Mediterranean Fish Dish
❧ with Feta Bruschetta Topping ❧

A super-fast and super-tasty way to dress up snoring, boring fish fillets, this mouthwatering skillet recipe works well with just about any type of fish, so use your favorite!

4 fish fillets, such as cod or haddock (5 oz/142 g each)

Sea salt and freshly ground black pepper

4 tsp olive oil, divided

2 tsp freshly squeezed lemon juice

½ cup minced red onions

2 tsp minced garlic

2 cups quartered grape tomatoes or diced Roma (plum) tomatoes

2 tsp balsamic vinegar

¼ cup crumbled light or regular feta cheese (1 oz/28 g)

12 basil leaves, thinly sliced or chopped

Pat fish dry with paper towels and sprinkle with salt and pepper on both sides. Heat 2 tsp olive oil in a 10-inch, nonstick skillet over medium-high heat. Add fish and cook for 2 to 3 minutes, or until edges start to brown. Carefully flip fish and cook about 2 more minutes or until fish is cooked through and flakes easily with a fork. Transfer fish to a serving plate, drizzle with lemon juice and keep warm.

Wipe skillet clean and heat remaining 2 tsp olive oil over medium-high heat. Add onions and garlic. Cook and stir until onions begin to soften and garlic turns golden, about 2 minutes. Stir in tomatoes, vinegar and a few grinds of salt and pepper. Mix well and cook 1 minute. Remove from heat and stir in feta and basil.

Spoon warm bruschetta over fish fillets and serve immediately.

Makes 4 servings

Per serving: 201 calories, 6.8 g total fat (1.5 g saturated fat), 28 g protein, 6.8 g carbohydrate (1.8 g fiber, 3.7 g sugars), 63 mg cholesterol, 314 mg sodium

SCAN FOR VIDEO!

YUM

Not a fan of feta? Use cubes of fresh mozzarella instead.

YUMMER!

Cook the fish in butter instead of olive oil. Extra tasty!

Bruschetta is BETTA with feta!

Crispy Baked Fish Sticks
～ with Greek Yogurt "Tartar" Sauce ～

My non-traditional tartar-like sauce uses Greek yogurt instead of mayonnaise since I always keep yogurt in my fridge but I rarely buy mayo. And there's no relish or pickles, either. So, it's not really tartar sauce, is it? Oh well, it's DILLicious! And when it comes to fish sticks, it's all about the dipping sauce, right?

Sauce

½ cup plain 0% Greek yogurt

1 tbsp grainy Dijon mustard

1 tbsp freshly squeezed lemon juice

1 tbsp minced fresh dill

1 tsp horseradish

1 tsp liquid honey or granulated sugar

½ tsp grated lemon zest

¼ tsp each sea salt and freshly ground
   black pepper

Fish

1½ lbs (680 g) cod, haddock or halibut
   fillets, about ½ inch thick

¾ cup cornflake crumbs or unseasoned
   bread crumbs

¼ cup finely grated Parmesan cheese

1 tsp Old Bay Seasoning*

¾ tsp dried thyme

½ tsp paprika

¼ tsp garlic powder

2 eggs, lightly beaten

½ cup whole wheat flour

Olive oil cooking spray or butter

* Look for Old Bay Seasoning in a yellow tin near the fish counter or in the spice aisle of your grocery store.

Preheat oven to 450°F. Spray a small baking sheet with cooking spray or lightly brush with oil. Set aside.

In a small bowl, combine yogurt, mustard, lemon juice, dill, horseradish, honey, lemon zest, salt and pepper. Mix well, cover and refrigerate until serving time.

Pat fish dry with paper towels, cut into 1 x 3-inch strips and set on a plate. Set up a dipping station with 3 shallow bowls or pie plates. In bowl 1, combine crumbs, Parmesan, Old Bay Seasoning, thyme, paprika and garlic powder. Place eggs in bowl 2 and flour in bowl 3. Working one at a time, dunk fish piece into flour, then into eggs (shake off excess), then into crumb mixture. Make sure fish is evenly coated with crumbs. Place on prepared pan and repeat with remaining fish pieces. This part's messy, I know.

Spray tops lightly with cooking spray (or drizzle with a bit of melted butter). Bake for 10 to 12 minutes, until fish is cooked through and breading is golden brown. Serve hot with tartar sauce.

Makes 4 generous servings

Per serving (with 2 tbsp sauce): 343 calories, 6.3 g total fat (2.3 g saturated fat), 41 g protein, 30 g carbohydrate (2.8 g fiber, 3.6 g sugars), 173 mg cholesterol, 690 mg sodium

SCAN FOR VIDEO!

GET HOOKED ON *fish!*

YUM
Use mayonnaise or sour cream instead of yogurt.

YUMMER!
Serve with Kaleslaw Salad, page 62.

Lickety-Split
Lemon-Butter Garlic Shrimp

GF

Your family will scampi* on over to the dinner table for this meal! Made in one skillet and ready in less than 20 minutes, you'll be amazed that something so simple can be so delicious.

3 tbsp butter, divided

1 tbsp minced garlic

1½ lbs (680 g) large raw shrimp, peeled and deveined (see Kitchen Whizdom)

Sea salt and freshly ground black pepper

2 tbsp freshly squeezed lemon juice

2 tbsp minced fresh parsley

* Yeah, I realize shrimp scampi contains wine and this recipe doesn't, but I couldn't resist the word play. Feel free to add a splash of white wine if you want!

In a 10-inch, non-stick skillet, heat 1 tbsp butter over medium heat until frothy. Add garlic. Cook and stir until garlic is golden and fragrant, about 1 minute. Don't rush it and don't burn it!

Pat shrimp dry with paper towels. Add shrimp and a few grinds of salt and pepper to skillet. Increase heat to medium-high. Cook and stir until shrimp turns pink and is opaque.

Add remaining 2 tbsp butter and lemon juice. Cook and stir until butter is melted, about 30 seconds. Remove from heat and stir in parsley. Serve immediately.

Makes 4 large or 6 small servings

Per serving (based on 4 servings): 261 calories, 11.2 g total fat (5.8 g saturated fat), 35 g protein, 3 g carbohydrate (0.2 g fiber, 0 g sugars), 281 mg cholesterol, 320 mg sodium

KITCHEN WHIZDOM

When it comes to shrimp, don't skimp! What I mean is don't buy small, wimpy shrimp for this recipe. You'll need large shrimp (about 20 to 25 per pound), but not jumbo (about 16 per pound), which I reserve for grilling or colossal shrimp cocktail. Frozen, raw shrimp is almost always on sale somewhere. Let the shrimp thaw, then remove the shells (and the tails if you want). Leaving the tails intact makes the shrimp look better (see photo!) and gives them built-in pink handles if you're eating with your fingers. However, unless you're feeding the Queen of England, taking a food photo or eating with your hands, I say lose the tails.

SCAN FOR VIDEO!

You are SO making this!

YUM
Like it hot? Add a pinch of crushed red pepper flakes when you add the salt and pepper.

YUMMER!
Serve with rice or pasta and a green veggie, like roasted asparagus or steamed broccoli.

Fabulous FISH TACOS

with Mango Salsa & Zesty Lime Mayo

GF **DF**

Fish tacos are often made with breaded or battered and fried fish, which is great for your taste buds but not for your waistline. This lighter, healthier, fresh and flavorful version is a meal I could scarf back every single day. Fish delish!

Mango Salsa

1½ cups diced mangos

1 small avocado, diced

½ cup diced red bell peppers

¼ cup finely minced red onions

2 tbsp minced jalapeño peppers

1 tbsp minced fresh cilantro

1 tbsp freshly squeezed lime juice

Pinch sea salt

Zesty Lime Mayo

⅓ cup light mayonnaise

1 tbsp freshly squeezed lime juice

½ tsp grated lime zest

⅛ tsp each chili powder and ground cumin

Fish

1½ lbs (680 g) mild white fish fillets, such as cod, mahi-mahi, halibut, haddock or tilapia*

2 tsp olive oil

Sea salt and freshly ground black pepper

1 tbsp freshly squeezed lime juice

8 small soft corn tortillas, warmed

Combine all salsa ingredients in a medium bowl and mix well. Cover and refrigerate until serving time. Same for the Zesty Lime Mayo: Whisk the ingredients together in a small bowl and pop it in the fridge.

Pat fish dry with paper towels and sprinkle both sides with salt and pepper. Heat olive oil in a 10-inch, nonstick skillet over medium-high heat. Add fish and cook for 2 to 3 minutes, or until edges start to look brown. Carefully flip fish and cook about 2 more minutes or until lightly browned and cooked through. Exact cooking time will depend on thickness of fish. Transfer fish to a serving plate and squeeze lime juice over top.

To assemble tacos, flake the fish or cut it into small pieces. Place fish over bottom of warmed tortillas, drizzle with lime mayo and top with salsa. Enjoy!

Makes 8 tacos

Per taco (with salsa and mayo): 196 calories, 5 g total fat (0.6 g saturated fat), 17 g protein, 21.3 g carbohydrate (3 g fiber, 5.4 g sugars), 37 mg cholesterol, 200 mg sodium

* Fish tacos are often made with tilapia, but I suffer from tilapi-phobia after buying and cooking tilapia that tasted exactly like swamp water. Yes, I once tasted swamp water, so I know. If you love tilapia (it's very popular!), go ahead and use it. ☺

YUM

No mayo? Use sour cream instead.

YUMMER!

Spice up the lime mayo by adding a shake or two of hot sauce.

Give 'em something to TACO 'bout!

SCAN FOR VIDEO!

Asian Tuna Burgers
❧ with Grilled Pineapple ❧

When it comes to burgers, sometimes I don't care where the beef is or I don't feel like talking turkey. That's when I crave this unique, fresh-tasting, aromatic tuna burger. (Aromatic. Did I just write that? Sorry. Cancelling my subscription to *Cuisine Queen* magazine immediately!)

1½ lbs (680 g) fresh tuna steaks

1 cup fresh bread crumbs (not dried;
  see Kitchen Whizdom)

1 egg

¼ cup finely minced green onions

2 tbsp hoisin sauce

2 tbsp minced fresh cilantro

2 tsp grated fresh gingerroot

1 tsp minced garlic

1 tsp dark sesame oil

½ tsp sea salt

¼ tsp freshly ground black pepper

6 slices fresh pineapple (½ inch thick)

1 large red onion, sliced into thick rings

Grainy, seedy buns or lettuce leaves
  (optional)

Makes 6 burgers

Per burger: 231 calories, 5.5 g total fat
(1 g saturated fat), 28 g protein, 16.8 g carbohydrate
(2.4 g fiber, 9 g sugars), 84 mg cholesterol,
348 mg sodium

Cut tuna into 1-inch chunks and place in the bowl of a food processor. Pulse on and off 4 or 5 times until tuna is coarsely ground. Transfer to a mixing bowl and add bread crumbs, egg, onions, hoisin sauce, cilantro, gingerroot, garlic, sesame oil, salt and pepper. Mix gently using your hands. Form tuna mixture into 6 patties, about ½ inch thick. Wet your hands to prevent sticking, if necessary. Place patties on a parchment-lined pan and stick it in the freezer while you grill the pineapple and onion rings.

Lightly oil a grill pan and place over medium-high heat. Grill pineapple and onion rings until onions have softened and both sides have nice grill marks. (Alternatively, use your outdoor gas barbecue, which I prefer for any type of grilling.) Cover and keep warm.

Re-oil the grill pan and cook burgers over medium-high heat for about 3 minutes per side, or until cooked to desired degree of doneness. Don't overcook tuna burgers or they'll be dry.

Serve hot patties topped with grilled pineapple and onion rings and any other condiments that suit your taste buds.

For this recipe, it's important that your bread crumbs are freshly made and that you don't use the standard, store-bought dried crumbs. Making fresh bread crumbs takes 30 seconds! Just place one or two slices of healthy, grainy bread in your food processor and pulse on and off until fluffy crumbs are formed.

 SCAN FOR VIDEO!

YUM
Try these burgers with
fresh salmon instead of tuna.

YUMMER!
Serve bunless with a side of
Crunchy Asian Slaw, page 54.

Where's the beef?
WHO CARES!

Lemony Salmon Bow-Tie Pasta
❧ with *Peas & Asparagus* ❧

This easy, cheesy salmon and pasta dinner-for-two takes no *skillet* all!
You *do* need a skillet, but not much skill—is what I'm sayin'.
Make this recipe when there's leftover cooked salmon in the fridge.

6 oz (170 g) uncooked bow-tie pasta
  (about 3 cups dry)
1 cup chopped fresh asparagus
¾ cup frozen green peas
2 tsp butter or olive oil
1 to 2 tsp minced garlic
1 cup 2% evaporated milk or 5% light cream
2 tsp all-purpose flour
¼ cup freshly grated Parmesan cheese
  + extra for serving
1 tbsp minced fresh dill
1 tbsp freshly squeezed lemon juice
1 tsp grated lemon zest
5 oz (142 g) cooked salmon, cut into chunks
Freshly ground black pepper

Cook pasta according to package directions, adding asparagus and peas during last 3 minutes of cooking time.

While pasta is cooking, prepare sauce. In a 10-inch, non-stick skillet, heat butter over medium heat until frothy. Add garlic. Cook and stir until garlic is golden and fragrant, about 1 minute. Be careful not to burn it.

In a small measuring cup, whisk together milk and flour until smooth with no lumps. Pour into skillet with garlic. Increase heat to medium-high, cook and stir until mixture bubbles and thickens slightly. Add cheese, dill, lemon juice and lemon zest. Mix well.

Drain pasta and vegetables and add them to the sauce, along with the salmon. Toss gently until all ingredients are coated with sauce. Serve immediately with freshly ground black pepper and extra Parmesan on top.

Makes 2 servings

Per serving: 598 calories, 14 g total fat (4 g saturated fat), 44 g protein, 86 g carbohydrate (6.4 g fiber, 19 g sugars), 85 mg cholesterol, 451 mg sodium

SCAN FOR VIDEO!

Wickedly Delicious
SPLURGE-WORTHY
Totally Worth It!

YUM
No leftover salmon in the fridge? A large can of wild salmon (drained!) will do!

YUMMER!
Try this recipe using leftover Roasted Whole Salmon Fillet, page 146. Fishalicious!

Thai Yellow Curry Shrimp
with Juicy Fresh Pineapple

I didn't think my love of Thai curries could grow stronger until a local chef threw some chunks of fresh pineapple in my "Curry of the Day" special. Sweet + heat is hard to beat!

2 tsp coconut oil or olive oil

1 cup coarsely chopped onions

1 cup thinly sliced red bell peppers

1 lb (454 g) large raw shrimp (20 to 25 per pound), peeled and deveined

2 tbsp Thai yellow (or red) curry paste (see Kitchen Whizdom)

1 tbsp grated fresh gingerroot

2 tsp minced garlic

1 can (14 oz/398 mL) coconut milk (light or regular)

1½ cups chopped fresh ripe pineapple

1 cup frozen shelled edamame beans, thawed

1 tbsp fish sauce (or reduced-sodium soy sauce*)

½ tsp grated lime zest

¼ cup coarsely chopped fresh cilantro or basil (or a bit of both)

Cooked basmati rice, jasmine rice or rice noodles (optional)

* For gluten-free, use Tamari soy sauce.

If you're serving this recipe with rice or noodles, get those started first. Have your ingredients prepped and ready to go as this meal comes together quickly.

Heat oil in a large, non-stick wok or skillet over medium-high heat. Add onions and peppers. Cook and stir until vegetables begin to soften, about 3 minutes. Stir in shrimp, curry paste, gingerroot and garlic. Cook and stir until shrimp turns pink and is almost (but not quite) opaque, about 3 minutes.

Add coconut milk, pineapple, edamame, fish sauce and lime zest. Mix well. Simmer, uncovered, for about 2 minutes, or until shrimp is cooked and pineapple is heated through. Remove from heat and stir in cilantro. Serve hot over rice or noodles, if using.

Makes 4 servings

Per serving (with light coconut milk; rice not included): 336 calories, 13 g total fat (8 g saturated fat), 29 g protein, 22 g carbohydrate (3.9 g fiber, 12 g sugars), 172 mg cholesterol, 667 mg sodium

Look for Thai curry paste (yellow, red or green) in small jars in the Asian or international food aisle of your grocery store. You really can't make Thai curries without the paste's distinct flavor, a combination of chili peppers, herbs and spices. The color depends on the type of chili pepper used, but I find all three varieties interchangeable in recipes. Don't confuse Thai curry with Indian curry! Completely different flavors! (I happen to love both.)

SCAN FOR VIDEO!

CURRY in a hurry!

YUM
Use green peas instead of edamame beans and mango instead of pineapple.

YUMMER!
Garnish with a few crushed cashews and extra cilantro or basil.

Spicy Chili-Lime Grilled Shrimp
➺ with Avocado Dipping Sauce ❧

Spicy shrimp + a cooling sauce = a palate-pleasing partnership! Sure to be a hit at your backyard barbecue party, this flavor-packed, marinated shrimp with creamy avocado dipping sauce can be served as a main course or as an appetizer.

Marinade

3 tbsp freshly squeezed lime juice

2 tbsp olive oil

1 tbsp liquid honey

2 tsp minced garlic

2 tsp chili powder

1 tsp ground cumin

1 tsp grated lime zest

½ tsp each paprika, sea salt and freshly ground black pepper

1½ lbs (680 g) jumbo raw shrimp (about 16 per pound), peeled and deveined

Dipping Sauce

1 medium ripe avocado

⅓ cup plain 0% Greek yogurt

2 tbsp minced fresh cilantro

4 to 6 metal skewers

In a small bowl or measuring cup, whisk together all marinade ingredients until well blended. Reserve 1 tbsp marinade to use in dipping sauce. Pour remaining marinade into a large, heavy-duty, resealable plastic bag. Add shrimp, seal bag and turn several times to coat shrimp evenly with marinade. Refrigerate for 30 minutes.

Meanwhile, make the dipping sauce. In a medium bowl, mash the avocado until smooth. Add yogurt, cilantro and reserved 1 tbsp marinade. Mix well, cover and refrigerate until serving time.

Preheat grill to medium-high setting. Thread shrimp onto skewers. Discard marinade. Brush grill rack lightly with oil. Grill shrimp for about 2 to 3 minutes per side, until pink and opaque. Serve hot with dipping sauce.

Makes 4 to 6 servings

Per serving (4 shrimp plus 2 tbsp sauce): 184 calories, 7.1 g total fat (1.1 g saturated fat), 24 g protein, 6 g carbohydrate (1.2 g fiber, 2.3 g sugars), 173 mg cholesterol, 328 mg sodium

Once the shrimp is on the grill, don't go fix yourself a cocktail or start up a game of lawn darts. Pay attention! Shrimp "meat" is quite sensitive to cooking time and temperature, changing from tender and juicy to overcooked and rubbery in the blink of an eye. (BTW, I have never been able to blink just one eye at a time. Useless Greta factoid #1.)

SCAN FOR VIDEO!

GRILLIN'
&
chillin'

YUM
This shrimp tastes
GREAT in tacos!

YUMMER!
Let's make a meal!
Serve with Grilled
Corn Salsa, page 210.

Roasted Whole Salmon Fillet
~ with Dill-icious Maple-Mustard Marinade ~

One of my most popular chicken recipes is called "Dilly Beloved," from my bestselling cookbook, *The Looneyspoons Collection*. (Shameless plug!) I could drink the marinade from a wine glass, it's so tasty! I've reduced the sweetness a bit, added more lemon and used it on a giant salmon fillet so you can feed a crowd. Enjoy!

1 large whole salmon fillet (about 3 lbs/1.4 kg; see Kitchen Whizdom)

Marinade

3 tbsp pure maple syrup

3 tbsp freshly squeezed lemon juice

3 tbsp grainy Dijon mustard

2 tbsp minced fresh dill

1 tbsp balsamic vinegar

1 tbsp olive oil

2 tsp grated lemon zest

1 tsp minced garlic

¼ tsp each sea salt and freshly ground black pepper

1 lemon, very thinly sliced

Spray a 9 x 13-inch baking dish with cooking spray or lightly oil. Place salmon fillet in baking dish and set aside.

In a small bowl or measuring cup, whisk together maple syrup, lemon juice, mustard, dill, vinegar, olive oil, lemon zest, garlic, salt and pepper. Pour over salmon and turn salmon to coat both sides with marinade. Arrange lemon slices over salmon. Cover and refrigerate for 1 to 2 hours.

Preheat oven to 425°F. Roast salmon (with marinade!), uncovered, for about 20 minutes, or until it's cooked through and flakes easily with a fork. Serve with roasted asparagus, steamed green beans, a rice side dish or a leafy green salad.

Makes 8 servings

Per serving: 239 calories, 11.2 g total fat (2 g saturated fat), 29 g protein, 4.6 g carbohydrate (0 g fiber, 4 g sugars), 78 mg cholesterol, 202 mg sodium

Ask the fishmonger (the seafood equivalent of a butcher) to cut a large piece of salmon for you, that way you'll get the exact size you want. Before roasting, I always fold the skinnier fillet ends under the thicker parts so the salmon cooks evenly. I prefer the look and taste of wild versus farmed salmon but *sheesh* it's expensive! Bonus: Wild salmon contains significantly fewer calories and less fat than farmed salmon. Must be all that open-water swimming!

SCAN FOR VIDEO!

Dinner party FAVORITE!

YUM
Tastes great cold, too! The perfect addition to leafy green salads.

YUMMER!
Leftovers? Use them in Lemony Salmon Bow-Tie Pasta, page 140.

CHAPTER 6

Fowl TERRITORY

Plate-lickin' chicken and
turkey recipes for gobbling!

YUM & YUMMER

Grilled Chicken Souvlaki
⤳ with Tzatziki Dipping Sauce ⤳

There's no need to wait for the Greek Food Festival to get your souvlaki fix! Perfect for a casual summer meal or for entertaining guests, these Mediterranean chicken kabobs with creamy tzatziki sauce are insanely easy to make and crazy delicious!

1½ lbs (680 g) boneless skinless chicken breasts

2 red bell peppers, cut into 1½-inch pieces

1 large red onion, cut into 1½-inch pieces

8 metal or wooden skewers*

Marinade

3 tbsp freshly squeezed lemon juice

2 tbsp olive oil

1 tbsp red wine vinegar

2 tsp minced garlic

1½ tsp dried oregano

1 tsp Dijon mustard

½ tsp dried Italian seasoning (or basil or thyme)

½ tsp each sea salt and freshly ground black pepper

Tzatziki Sauce

1 cup plain 0% Greek yogurt

¾ cup peeled, finely diced English cucumbers

1 tbsp freshly squeezed lemon juice

1 tbsp minced fresh dill

2 tsp liquid honey**

1 tsp minced garlic

¼ tsp each sea salt and freshly ground black pepper

* If using wooden skewers, soak them in cold water for at least an hour before using to prevent burning.

** The honey doesn't make the sauce sweet, it just lessens the tang of the Greek yogurt. Feel free to leave it out.

Cut chicken into 1½-inch chunks and set aside.

In a large bowl, whisk together all marinade ingredients until well blended. Add chicken pieces and stir to coat evenly with marinade. Cover with plastic wrap and refrigerate for 2 to 4 hours.

While chicken is marinating, make tzatziki sauce. Combine all sauce ingredients in a medium bowl and mix well. Cover and refrigerate until serving time.

Preheat grill to medium-high heat. Thread chicken, bell peppers and onions onto skewers as pictured in photo, beginning and ending with chicken. Gah! I hate this part. Kinda messy. But worth it.

Lightly oil grill racks. Place skewers on racks and grill for 10 to 12 minutes, turning occasionally to ensure even cooking. Serve hot with tzatziki sauce.

Makes 8 skewers

Per skewer (with ¼ cup sauce): 167 calories, 3.6 g total fat (0.6 g saturated fat), 24 g protein, 10 g carbohydrate (1.8 g fiber, 5 g sugars), 52 mg cholesterol, 266 mg sodium

SCAN FOR VIDEO!

It's all GREEK to me!

YUM
For a less tangy tzatziki, use sour cream instead of Greek yogurt.

YUMMER!
Serve with lightly grilled, whole-grain pita bread, hummus and a leafy green salad for a fabulous Greek-style feast!

Indian Coconut Curry Chicken Thighs
with Sweet Potatoes & Green Peas

Fragrant and fantastic, this one-pot wonderful, super-savory supper can be made in about 30 minutes. Serve on a bed of brown basmati rice, quinoa or whole wheat couscous.

1 tbsp olive oil

10 large boneless skinless chicken thighs
(about 2¼ lbs/1 kg)

1½ cups chopped onions

2 tsp minced garlic

1 tbsp grated fresh gingerroot

1 tbsp curry powder

1 tbsp garam masala spice blend
(see Kitchen Whizdom, page 222)

1 can (14 oz/398 mL) coconut milk
(light or regular)

3 tbsp tomato paste

2 tsp brown sugar (optional)

½ tsp sea salt

1½ cups peeled, diced sweet potatoes

1 cup green peas (fresh or frozen)

2 tbsp minced fresh cilantro

You'll need a large (12-inch), non-stick skillet with a lid for this recipe.

Heat olive oil in the skillet over medium-high heat. Add chicken pieces and brown on both sides. Remove chicken from skillet and set aside.

To the same skillet, add onions and garlic. Reduce heat to medium. Cook and stir until onions begin to soften, about 3 to 4 minutes. Add gingerroot, curry powder and garam masala. Mix well and cook for 30 seconds. Add coconut milk, tomato paste, brown sugar, if using, and salt. Cook and stir until mixture is bubbly and well blended. Stir in sweet potatoes.

Return chicken pieces to skillet and spoon sauce over top. It won't look very pretty at this point but hang in there. Reduce heat to low. Cover and simmer for 15 minutes.

Stir in green peas and cook for 5 more minutes, just until peas are heated through. Sprinkle with cilantro and serve hot.

Makes 4 to 5 servings

Per serving (based on 5 servings using light coconut milk): 388 calories, 16 g total fat (6 g saturated fat), 39 g protein, 20 g carbohydrate (3.7 g fiber, 8.7 g sugars), 151 mg cholesterol, 445 mg sodium

SCAN FOR VIDEO!

YUM

Prefer chicken breasts? Cut them into thirds and use instead of thighs. Reduce simmering time by 5 minutes.

YUMMER!

Like really spicy food? Add ¼ tsp (or more) cayenne pepper.

One-Pot Wonderful!

Mediterranean Turkey Burgers
with Feta & Spinach

GF

These mouthwatering turkey burgers get their Mediterranean flair from the addition of feta cheese, sun-dried tomato pesto and spinach. They're delicious topped with tzatziki, hummus, sliced tomatoes and/or cucumbers, sprouts or even zesty tomato sauce.

⅔ cup quick-cooking oats (not instant)

1½ lbs (680 g) ground turkey

½ cup finely chopped cooked spinach
 (see Kitchen Whizdom)

⅓ cup crumbled light or regular feta cheese
 (1½ oz/43 g)

1 egg

2 tbsp sun-dried tomato pesto

½ tsp freshly ground black pepper

Sea salt to taste

In the bowl of a food processor or blender, process the oats until they're the consistency of bread crumbs (but no powdery). Place oats and ground turkey in a large bowl with all remaining ingredients. Mix gently using your hands until all ingredients are well incorporated. Form mixture into 5 large patties or 6 smaller patties. Cover with plastic wrap and refrigerate while you preheat the grill to medium-high heat.

Lightly oil grill rack. Grill burgers for 5 to 6 minutes per side, or until cooked through and no longer pink in the center. Serve on multigrain buns or with grilled portobello "buns" (eat with a knife and fork!) to keep them gluten-free.

Makes 5 large burgers or 6 regular-sized burgers

Per burger (based on 6 burgers): 227 calories, 11 g total fat (3.5 g saturated fat), 26 g protein, 8 g carbohydrate (1.9 g fiber, 0.5 g sugars), 129 mg cholesterol, 272 mg sodium

If using frozen spinach, thaw it and squeeze dry before chopping and adding to the recipe. To make portobello "buns," simply brush large portobello mushroom caps with olive oil on both sides and grill alongside the burgers.

SCAN FOR VIDEO!

Portobello "BUNS"

YUM
Try basil pesto instead
of sun-dried tomato pesto.

YUMMER!
Use the turkey mixture to make
meatballs and serve with tomato sauce.

Chicken & Wild Mushroom Skillet
❧ with Asiago Cream Sauce ❧

Fancy enough for company, but easy enough for busy weeknights, since you'll be devouring juicy chicken with gourmet flavor in under 30 minutes. Serve with a green veggie and something starchy to soak up the scrumptious sauce (brown and wild rice, quinoa, mashed potatoes, pasta, etc.).

4 boneless skinless chicken breasts (about 1½ lbs/680 g), pounded to even thickness

Sea salt and freshly ground black pepper

1 tbsp olive oil

1 tbsp butter (or more olive oil)

1 cup diced onions

1 tsp minced garlic

8 oz (227 g) mixed wild mushrooms, sliced*

1 tbsp minced fresh thyme

1 cup reduced-sodium chicken broth

⅓ cup dry white wine

1 tbsp grainy Dijon mustard

⅓ cup heavy (whipping) cream

2 tsp cornstarch

⅓ cup freshly grated Asiago cheese (about 1½ oz/43 g)

* I use a combination of cremini and shiitake mushrooms for this recipe.

Lightly sprinkle both sides of chicken breasts with salt and pepper. Heat olive oil in a 10-inch, non-stick skillet over medium-high heat. Add chicken. Cook for 2 to 3 minutes per side, until lightly browned. Remove chicken from skillet and keep warm.

Return skillet to heat and add butter. When melted, add onions and garlic. Cook and stir until onions begin to soften, about 2 minutes. Add mushrooms and cook until mushrooms are tender, stirring often, about 5 minutes. Stir in thyme and cook for 1 more minute.

Add broth, wine, mustard and a few grinds of black pepper. Mix well. Bring mixture to a gentle boil, then reduce heat to low. Add browned chicken. Cover with a lid and cook for about 10 minutes, until chicken is fully cooked and no longer pink in the center. Remove chicken from pan (yup, again!) and keep warm.

In a small measuring cup, whisk together cream and cornstarch until smooth. Pour into skillet with mushroom sauce. Increase heat to medium-high, cook and stir until mixture is bubbly and has thickened slightly. Add Asiago and stir until melted. Serve hot mushroom sauce over chicken.

Makes 4 servings

Per serving: 408 calories, 19 g total fat (9.4 g saturated fat), 45 g protein, 9.5 g carbohydrate (1 g fiber, 2.9 g sugars), 141 mg cholesterol, 486 mg sodium

SCAN FOR VIDEO!

Wickedly Delicious
SPLURGE-WORTHY
Totally Worth It!

#awesomesauce #pantastic

Chicken Penne Florentine
~ with Roasted Tomato Pesto ~

Dinner's ready in under 30 minutes when you whip up this high-fiber, high-flavor, comforting chicken and penne stir-fry. The homemade tomato pesto is the besto, but you can certainly use your favorite store-bought pesto instead.

12 oz (340 g) gluten-free or
  whole wheat penne noodles

1 tbsp olive oil

1 large red bell pepper, thinly sliced

1 medium red onion, sliced

3 small handfuls baby spinach

2 cups sliced or cubed cooked chicken breast
  (see Kitchen Whizdom)

⅓ cup Roasted Tomato Pesto (see recipe,
  page 116)

Freshly grated Parmesan cheese and freshly
  ground black pepper for serving (optional)

In a large pot, cook penne noodles according to package directions or until al dente.

While pasta is cooking, heat olive oil in a deep, 12-inch, non-stick skillet over medium-high heat. Add bell peppers and onions. Cook and stir until vegetables are tender, about 5 minutes. Add spinach and ¼ cup water. Cook and stir until spinach is wilted and water has evaporated, about 2 minutes.

Reduce heat to low. Add drained pasta to skillet along with chicken and pesto. Toss until all ingredients are coated with pesto. If you like more pesto, add more pesto! You can adjust this recipe to suit your tastes. Sprinkle with Parmesan and pepper before serving, if desired.

Makes 4 servings

Per serving: 486 calories, 15 g total fat (2.6 g saturated fat), 33 g protein, 60 g carbohydrate (11 g fiber, 4 g sugars), 52 mg cholesterol, 227 mg sodium

I love recipe shortcuts, especially when I'm really busy or really hungry! This recipe calls for pre-cooked chicken but, if you prefer, you can stir-fry cubed raw chicken at the start of the recipe. Personally, I love using sliced rotisserie chicken breasts to save time. You can also use cooked chicken breast slices found in the deli section of most grocery stores—but check for natural ingredients, no preservatives and a reasonable amount of sodium. If you love the taste of bacon, chop up 4 slices of nitrate-free bacon and cook them in the skillet before adding the peppers and onions.

SCAN FOR VIDEO!

YUM

Try basil pesto instead of roasted tomato pesto. Start with ¼ cup basil pesto and work your way up from there.

YUMMER!

Think adding bacon to this recipe would make it taste incredible? You're right! See Kitchen Whizdom for how-to.

THIS PENNE'S ♥ from heaven!

Cheesy Caprese Chicken
with Roasted Tomatoes

GF

The popular Italian Caprese salad is the inspiration for this mouthwatering, slightly decadent, company-worthy chicken entrée. Roasting the tomatoes makes them taste like vegetable candy!

1 lb (454 g) small Roma (plum) tomatoes, quartered (6 to 8 tomatoes)

2 tbsp olive oil, divided

Sea salt and freshly ground black pepper

4 large boneless skinless chicken breasts (about 1½ to 2 lbs/680 to 907 g), pounded to even thickness

4 to 6 oz (113 to 170 g) fresh mozzarella cheese, drained and cut into ¼-inch-thick slices

2 tbsp balsamic reduction (store-bought or homemade; see Kitchen Whizdom)

¼ cup chopped fresh basil

Makes 4 servings

Per serving: 359 calories, 15 g total fat (5 g saturated fat), 41 g protein, 15 g carbohydrate (1.4 g fiber, 9.5 g sugars), 115 mg cholesterol, 270 mg sodium

Line a 10 x 15-inch, rimmed baking sheet with parchment paper. Arrange tomatoes in a single layer on pan, cut-side up. Drizzle with 1 tbsp olive oil and a pinch of salt and pepper. You can use your hands to mix the tomatoes and the oil, but make sure you put them back in a tidy, single layer please.

Roast tomatoes at 400°F for 30 to 40 minutes, or until they appear lightly caramelized and edges begin to brown. Crank on the broiler for a minute or two to get that last bit of browning magic, then remove tomatoes from oven.

While tomatoes are roasting, prepare chicken. Heat remaining 1 tbsp olive oil in a large, non-stick skillet over medium-high heat. Sprinkle chicken lightly with salt and pepper. Add chicken to pan and cook until lightly browned on one side. Flip the chicken breasts over, reduce heat to low and cover skillet with a lid. Make sure heat is low and lid fits snuggly. Cook chicken for 15 minutes. Remove from heat and let chicken rest in covered skillet for 5 minutes.

Carefully spoon off and discard liquid from skillet and return chicken to stovetop over low heat. Top each chicken breast with fresh mozzarella, followed by roasted tomatoes. Cover with lid and let stand 2 to 3 minutes, until cheese is melted. Drizzle with balsamic reduction, then sprinkle with chopped basil. Top with freshly ground black pepper, if desired.

KITCHEN WHIZDOM

To make balsamic reduction, whisk together ⅓ cup balsamic vinegar and 1 tbsp sweetener of choice (honey, maple syrup, coconut sugar, brown sugar, granulated sugar) in a small pot over medium-high heat. Bring mixture to a gentle boil, then reduce heat to low. Simmer (uncovered) until mixture gets syrupy and reduces in quantity by about half (5 minutes max), whisking occasionally. It'll thicken a bit as it cools, so keep this in mind. If you thicken it too much, you can always thin it with water. Cool slightly before using.

SCAN FOR VIDEO!

Bursting with roasted tomato-ness!

YUM
Instead of plum tomatoes, use "cocktail" or Campari tomatoes (love these!).

YUMMER!
Serve with a garden salad or green veggies such as roasted asparagus or steamed green beans.

Coconut Tandoori

1 cup coconut milk (regular, not light)

2 tbsp freshly squeezed lime juice

1 tbsp each paprika, ground cumin,
   ground coriander and garam masala
   spice blend*

1 tbsp minced garlic

1 tbsp grated fresh gingerroot

1 tsp chili powder

1 tsp grated lime zest

½ tsp sea salt

¼ tsp cayenne pepper

* See Kitchen Whizdom, page 222.

HONEY GARLIC & Ginger

3 tbsp liquid honey

1 tbsp molasses

2 tbsp reduced-sodium soy sauce
  (use Tamari soy sauce for gluten-free)

2 tbsp freshly squeezed lemon juice

2 tbsp finely minced green onions (with white parts)

1 tbsp minced garlic

1 tbsp grated fresh gingerroot

½ tsp each sea salt and crushed red pepper flakes

Happily
MARINATED CHICKEN

Cuz tasteless poultry is for the birds!

Directions:

Whisk together all marinade ingredients in a small bowl. Pour over 2 lbs (907 g) chicken pieces, turn pieces to coat evenly with marinade, cover and refrigerate for at least 2 hours. Preheat oven to 375°F. Bake thighs and drumsticks for 40 to 45 minutes or breasts for 30 to 35 minutes.

GF DF

Maple, Balsamic & Rosemary

¼ cup pure maple syrup

3 tbsp freshly squeezed lemon juice

2 tbsp grainy Dijon mustard

2 tbsp balsamic vinegar

1 tbsp olive oil

1 tbsp minced fresh rosemary

2 tsp minced garlic

1½ tsp grated lemon zest

½ tsp each sea salt and freshly ground black pepper

See page 285 for Nutritional Info.

SCAN FOR VIDEO!

Lip-Smacking
Maple-Curry Chicken

GF DF

How could something so easy be so delicious? That's the question I ask myself every time I make this simple yet sensational baked chicken recipe. Warning: Be careful not to burn your face when it's pressed against your oven's glass window. (You know, as you count down the seconds 'til dinnertime!)

>>

Marinade

⅓ **cup pure maple syrup**

¼ **cup grainy Dijon mustard**

1 **tbsp reduced-sodium soy sauce**
 (use Tamari soy sauce for gluten-free)

1 **tbsp curry powder (see Kitchen Whizdom)**

2 **tsp minced garlic**

½ **tsp each ground cumin, chili powder**
 and freshly ground black pepper

¼ **tsp each sea salt and cayenne pepper**

6 **chicken drumsticks (about 1½ lbs/680 g)***

6 **bone-in chicken thighs (about 1½ lbs/680 g)***

* You can take the skin off or leave it on.
It's up to you!

In a large bowl, whisk together all marinade ingredients until well blended. Add chicken pieces and turn to coat evenly with marinade. Cover with plastic wrap and refrigerate for at least 2 hours or up to 24 hours.

Preheat oven to 375°F. Arrange chicken pieces in a single layer on a large, rimmed baking sheet (line with parchment paper for easier cleanup). Drizzle extra marinade over each piece. Bake in preheated oven for 40 to 45 minutes or until chicken is cooked through. Serve hot.

Makes 6 servings

Per serving (without skin): 241 calories, 9.8 g total fat (3 g saturated fat), 27 g protein, 10 g carbohydrate (0.5 g fiber, 9 g sugars), 90 mg cholesterol, 400 mg sodium

The term "curry powder" means different things to different people. But to me (and this recipe), it means a vibrant yellow spice mix that most often includes cumin, coriander, turmeric, ginger, cardamom and cayenne, among other tasty, awesome spices. I'd rank curry powder in my top 5 list of must-have spices for flavorful, healthy cooking. Thankfully, pre-fab curry powder is available everywhere, so you don't need to make your own blend (though you certainly could). The ingredients and heat factor vary among brands, so it might take a couple tries to find the curry blend you love most.

SCAN FOR VIDEO!

YUM
Use 6 small chicken breasts instead of thighs. Reduce baking time to 30 to 35 minutes.

YUMMER!
This marinade is exceptionally tasty on salmon fillets!

MY FLAVORITE *chicken marinade!*

Chicken Enchilada Casserole
≫ with Black Beans & Butternut Squash ≪

GF*

If you're obsessed with Mexican food like I am, this sinfully delicious recipe is for you! It's surprisingly easy to make, since it uses helpful shortcuts like rotisserie chicken and pre-shredded cheese. The addition of butternut squash is pure genius! (Translation: I did not come up with this idea. Sigh.)

Sauce

1 tbsp olive oil

1 cup diced onions

2 tsp minced garlic

1 can (23 oz/680 mL) no-salt-added tomato sauce

1½ cups reduced-sodium chicken broth

1½ tbsp chili powder

1 tsp ground cumin

½ tsp dried oregano

¼ tsp sea salt

2 tbsp minced fresh cilantro

12 7-inch corn or flour tortillas*

4 cups chopped cooked rotisserie chicken (light and dark meat)

1 can (19 oz/540 mL) no-salt-added black beans, drained and rinsed

2 cups diced butternut squash

2 cups shredded part-skim Tex-Mex cheese blend (8 oz/227 g)

Optional garnishes: Diced avocados, chopped green onions, diced tomatoes and minced fresh cilantro

* For gluten-free, use 100% corn flour tortillas.

Heat olive oil in a medium pot over medium-high heat. Add onions and garlic. Cook and stir until onions begin to soften, about 2 minutes. Stir in tomato sauce, broth, chili powder, cumin, oregano and salt. Mix well. Bring mixture to a boil. Reduce heat to low and simmer, uncovered, for 5 minutes. Remove sauce from heat and stir in cilantro.

Preheat oven to 375°F. Spray a deep, 9 x 13-inch casserole dish with cooking spray or lightly oil. Spoon about ¾ cup sauce over bottom of dish. Top with 3 tortillas, cutting as necessary to make them fit. Top tortillas with another ¾ cup sauce followed by ⅓ chicken, ⅓ beans, ⅓ squash and ¼ cheese. Repeat layering two more times: 3 tortillas, ¾ cup sauce, ⅓ chicken, ⅓ beans, ⅓ squash and ¼ cheese. Top with remaining 3 tortillas, followed by remaining sauce and cheese.

Spray foil with cooking spray (or lightly oil) and cover casserole dish. Bake in preheated oven for 40 minutes. Uncover and bake for another 10 minutes. Let casserole stand, uncovered, for 10 minutes before serving. Serve hot with any or all of the optional garnishes.

Makes 8 servings

Per serving: 478 calories, 15.7 g total fat (3.5 g saturated fat), 37 g protein, 46 g carbohydrate (7.8 g fiber, 5.9 g sugars), 78 mg cholesterol, 617 mg sodium

SCAN FOR VIDEO!

Dinner tonight!

YUM
Not a fan of squash?
Use drained, canned
corn instead.

YUMMER!
A dollop of sour cream
or guacamole (or both)
on top would make this
casserole doubly delicious.

Indian-Spiced Chicken Drumsticks
with Cucumber-Mint Yogurt Sauce

GF

Oven-roasted chicken marinated in fragrant, warm spices gets paired with popular Indian "raita" sauce for an incredible, unforgettable dinner!

Marinade

¼ cup olive oil

2 tbsp freshly squeezed lemon juice

1 tbsp liquid honey

1 tbsp grated fresh gingerroot

2 tsp each ground cumin, ground coriander and curry powder

2 tsp minced garlic

1 tsp grated lemon zest

½ tsp each paprika, sea salt and freshly ground black pepper

¼ tsp each cayenne pepper and ground cinnamon

12 chicken drumsticks (about 3 lbs/1.4 kg)*

Yogurt Sauce

1 English cucumber, peeled and grated**

1 cup plain 0% Greek yogurt

2 tbsp minced fresh mint

1 tbsp freshly squeezed lemon juice

1 tsp liquid honey

½ tsp grated lemon zest

½ tsp sea salt

¼ tsp each ground cumin and freshly ground black pepper

* You can take the skin off or leave it on. It's up to you!

** The grated cucumber must be squeezed dry before adding it to the yogurt, otherwise the sauce will be very runny. Use a clean tea towel or paper towels for this job.

Whisk together all marinade ingredients in a small bowl. Pour over chicken in a glass baking dish or in a large, heavy-duty, resealable plastic bag. Make sure chicken is evenly coated with marinade. Marinate in refrigerator for at least 3 hours or overnight.

About an hour before serving, make the sauce. Combine all sauce ingredients in a medium bowl. Mix well. Cover and refrigerate until serving time. Allowing an hour for the ingredients to mingle in the fridge improves the sauce's flavor.

Preheat oven to 375°F. Arrange chicken pieces in a single layer on a large, rimmed baking sheet (line with parchment paper for easier cleanup). Drizzle any extra marinade over top. Bake in preheated oven for about 40 to 45 minutes, depending on size of drumsticks, or until no longer pink in the center. Turn on the broiler and broil for about 1 minute until chicken is lightly browned. Serve with yogurt sauce on the side.

Makes 12 drumsticks and 1½ cups yogurt sauce

Per serving (based on 2 drumsticks without skin): 229 calories, 12 g total fat (2.3 g saturated fat), 25 g protein, 4 g carbohydrate (0 g fiber, 2.1 g sugars), 82 mg cholesterol, 217 mg sodium

Yogurt Sauce (per ¼ cup): 37 calories, 1 g total fat (0.5 g saturated fat), 4 g protein, 3.7 g carbohydrate (0.7 g fiber, 2.9 g sugars), 3 mg cholesterol, 193 mg sodium

SCAN FOR VIDEO!

YUMMY DRUMMIES!

YUM
Use chicken thighs instead of drumsticks.

YUMMER!
The yogurt sauce tastes GREAT with Coconut Tandoori Chicken, page 162.

Thai Red Curry Chicken
with Vegetables

GF **DF**

Fast, fresh and flavorful! This delicious Thai stir-fry can be made in less than 30 minutes, so it's perfect for busy weeknights. Serve with jasmine or basmati rice to soak up the amazing sauce.

1 tbsp coconut oil or peanut oil

1¼ lbs (567 g) boneless skinless chicken breasts (or thighs), cut into strips or cubes

1 medium onion, chopped

2 tsp grated fresh gingerroot

2 tsp minced garlic

2 baby eggplants, cut into cubes (or about 2 cups chopped eggplant)

1 small handful sugar snap peas or snow peas

1 medium red bell pepper, cut into strips

2 tbsp Thai red curry paste (see Kitchen Whizdom)

1 can (14 oz/398 mL) coconut milk (light or regular)

1 tbsp fish sauce (or reduced-sodium soy sauce*)

1 tbsp coconut sugar or brown sugar

1 tbsp freshly squeezed lime juice

½ tsp grated lime zest

15 fresh basil leaves

3 tbsp chopped fresh cilantro

* For gluten-free, use Tamari soy sauce.

If you're serving this recipe with jasmine or basmati rice, get that started first. Have your ingredients prepped and ready to go as this meal comes together quickly.

Heat coconut oil in a large, non-stick wok or skillet over medium-high heat. Add chicken. Cook and stir until chicken is lightly browned and almost cooked through. Remove from skillet and set aside.

Add onions, gingerroot and garlic to skillet. (Add a bit more oil or some water, if necessary, to prevent sticking.) Cook and stir until onions begin to soften, about 3 minutes. Add eggplants, sugar snap peas and bell peppers. Continue stir-frying for about 5 more minutes. Stir in curry paste and cook for 30 more seconds.

Return chicken to skillet, along with coconut milk, fish sauce, sugar, lime juice and zest. Mix well and bring to a gentle boil. Reduce heat to medium and let mixture cook, uncovered, for about 5 minutes, until chicken is cooked through. Stir in basil and cilantro. Serve hot.

Makes 4 servings

Per serving (with light coconut milk; rice not included): 342 calories, 12.6 g total fat (8.8 g saturated fat), 36 g protein, 18 g carbohydrate (4 g fiber, 10 g sugars), 82 mg cholesterol, 703 mg sodium

Thai red curry paste and fish sauce are essential ingredients in this recipe. Look for the paste in a small jar and the fish sauce in a bottle in the ethnic or international food aisle of your grocery store. In a pinch, you can substitute soy sauce for the fish sauce but the flavor won't be quite the same. It's still good though! With Thai curry, just about any type of vegetable works: broccoli, mini corn cobs, baby bok choy, green beans—even small cubes of squash or sweet potatoes. Have fun with it!

SCAN FOR VIDEO!

Thai it! You'll like it!

YUM
Try zucchini instead of eggplant and shrimp instead of chicken.

YUMMER!
Using full-fat coconut milk makes this dish extra rich and creamy!

Honey, Lime & Sriracha Grilled Chicken
⊷ with Grilled Pineapple Salsa ⊶

This chicken is dressed to grill! A little bit sweet and a little bit spicy, this flavorful marinade with honey, lime, Asian chili sauce (Sriracha), fresh gingerroot and spices transforms boring chicken thighs or drumsticks into barbecued deliciousness!

Marinade

¼ cup liquid honey

¼ cup freshly squeezed lime juice

2 tbsp reduced-sodium soy sauce
  (use Tamari soy sauce for gluten-free)

2 tbsp Sriracha hot sauce

1 tbsp olive oil

2 tsp grated lime zest

2 tsp minced garlic

2 tsp grated fresh gingerroot

½ tsp each ground cumin and chili powder

8 large bone-in chicken thighs,
  skin removed (about 2 lbs/907 g)

Salsa

1 whole (ripe!) fresh pineapple, peeled,
  cored and sliced into 6 thick rings

1 medium red bell pepper, halved,
  seeds removed

⅓ cup minced red onions

1 jalapeño pepper, minced

2 tbsp freshly squeezed lime juice

1 to 2 tbsp minced fresh cilantro

Pinch sea salt

Whisk together all marinade ingredients in a small bowl or measuring cup. Reserve ¼ cup marinade to use as a basting sauce for chicken while grilling. Pour remaining marinade (about ½ cup) over chicken thighs in a small glass baking dish. Turn chicken pieces over several times to coat evenly with marinade. Cover with plastic wrap and marinate in the fridge for at least 8 hours or overnight.

Just before grilling chicken, make the salsa. Preheat grill to medium-high heat and lightly oil grill racks. Place pineapple rings and bell pepper halves on grill. Close lid. Cook for about 4 minutes per side, until heated through with nice grill marks on the surface. Remove from heat.

When cool enough to handle, dice pineapple and bell pepper and place in a medium bowl. Add remaining salsa ingredients and mix well. Let salsa stand at room temperature while you grill the chicken.

Reduce grill heat to medium. Re-oil grill racks if desired. Grill chicken thighs for about 10 minutes per side with lid closed. Baste generously with reserved marinade during last 2 minutes of cooking time. Serve hot with pineapple salsa.

Makes 4 servings

Per serving (with ½ cup salsa): 366 calories, 10.7 g total fat (2.3 g saturated fat), 41 g protein, 27 g carbohydrate (1.5 g fiber, 20 g sugars), 166 mg cholesterol, 516 mg sodium

SCAN FOR VIDEO!

Honey Mustard & Herb Roasted Chicken

This super-tasty chicken is truly finger-lickin' and so easy to make. Whip together the marinade, let the chicken soak in it for a few hours, then bake and devour! Serve this chicken with a green veggie and a potato, rice or quinoa side dish.

Marinade

¼ cup liquid honey

¼ cup grainy Dijon mustard

3 tbsp freshly squeezed lemon juice

1 tbsp balsamic vinegar

1 tbsp olive oil

2 tsp minced garlic

2 tsp each minced fresh thyme and rosemary
 (see Kitchen Whizdom)

1 tsp grated lemon zest

½ tsp sea salt

¼ tsp freshly ground black pepper

5 large bone-in chicken thighs, skin on*
 (about 1½ lbs/680 g)

5 large chicken drumsticks
 (about 1¼ lbs/567 g)

1 small lemon, thinly sliced

* To lower the fat content, you can remove
the chicken skin.

Whisk together all marinade ingredients in a small bowl or measuring cup. Place chicken pieces in a large, heavy-duty, resealable plastic bag. Add marinade and seal bag. Turn bag several times to coat chicken evenly with marinade. Refrigerate for at least 3 hours.

Preheat oven to 375°F. Coat a 9 x 13-inch baking pan or casserole dish with cooking spray (or line with foil). Arrange chicken pieces in pan and pour marinade over chicken. Make sure chicken pieces aren't overlapping. Scatter lemon slices over top. Bake in preheated oven for 45 minutes, or until chicken is cooked through and lightly browned on top. Delish!

Makes 5 servings

Per serving (1 drumstick, 1 thigh, with skin): 299 calories, 18 g total fat (5 g saturated fat), 26 g protein, 8 g carbohydrate (0.2 g fiber, 6.7 g sugars), 93 mg cholesterol, 311 mg sodium

I love this chicken dish and so does everyone else! The flavor is similar to the Maple Balsamic & Rosemary chicken marinade on page 163, but this recipe is made with honey and it's more mustardy. Thus, the "honey mustard" in the title. ☺ Fresh thyme and rosemary are SO nice in this marinade, but if you must use dried, reduce the quantity to 1 tsp each.

SCAN FOR VIDEO!

This top-rated recipe gets rave reviews!

Asian Chicken Lettuce Wraps
with Hidden Veggies

**Healthy, simple and fun to make, these low-carb "Asian tacos" are ready in about 20 minutes.
Plus, they're easy on the wallet and everyone loves 'em. Lettuce rejoice!**

Sauce

⅓ **cup hoisin sauce***

2 **tbsp rice vinegar**

2 **tbsp reduced-sodium soy sauce***

1 **tsp dark sesame oil**

1 **tsp minced garlic**

1 **tsp grated fresh gingerroot**

Filling

2 **tsp olive oil**

1 **lb (454 g) ground chicken**

½ **cup diced onions**

½ **cup minced zucchini**

½ **cup minced cremini or shiitake mushrooms**

½ **cup minced water chestnuts**

1 **head Boston lettuce, leaves separated**

Garnishes

Toasted sesame seeds

Cucumber strips

Chopped green onions

Fresh cilantro

* For gluten-free, use GF hoisin sauce and
Tamari soy sauce.

In a small bowl or measuring cup, whisk together all sauce ingredients and set them aside to mingle while you prepare the filling.

Heat olive oil in a 10-inch, non-stick skillet over medium-high heat. Add chicken. Cook and stir until chicken is lightly browned, breaking apart any large chunks of chicken as it's cooking.

Add onions, zucchini and mushrooms. Cook and stir until vegetables are tender, about 3 minutes. (You chopped them super small, right?) Stir in water chestnuts and reserved sauce. Cook and stir until sauce is heated through. Remove chicken mixture from heat.

To serve, place several spoonfuls of filling onto a lettuce leaf (layer two leaves if they're on the small side). Top with garnishes (I love the cucumber strips!), fold sides over and devour.

Makes 12 lettuce wraps

Per wrap: 89 calories, 4 g total fat (1 g saturated fat), 7.9 g protein, 6 g carbohydrate (0.7 g fiber, 3 g sugars), 34 mg cholesterol, 237 mg sodium

SCAN FOR VIDEO!

YUM
Try this recipe with extra-lean ground beef instead of chicken.

YUMMER!
Feeling super hungry? Wrap filling in warm, mini flour tortillas instead of lettuce.

Low carb, high taste!

CHAPTER 7

Meat
LOVERS

Stick your fork in some beef and pork!

YUM & YUMMER

✎ Mucho Yummy ✎
Beef Bowlrito

GF

A healthy version of a restaurant favorite, this big bowla Mexican deliciousness is basically a burrito without the tortilla! Customize your bowlrito by choosing from an assortment of tasty toppings.

Cilantro-Lime Rice

2 cups hot cooked brown rice

1 tbsp freshly squeezed lime juice

1 tbsp minced fresh cilantro

½ tsp grated lime zest

Spiced Beef

1¼ lbs (567 g) extra-lean ground beef

½ cup diced onions

1 tsp minced garlic

¼ cup ketchup

¼ cup water

2 tbsp taco seasoning (store-bought or homemade; see recipe, page 38)

Toppings

Corn	**Shredded cheese**
Black beans	**Chopped green onions**
Salsa	**Fresh cilantro**
Guacamole	
Greek yogurt or sour cream	

Combine hot rice with lime juice, cilantro and lime zest and keep warm. (Mix everything in the rice cooking pot and put the lid back on until you're ready to assemble bowlritos.)

Heat a 10-inch, non-stick skillet over medium-high heat. Add beef, onions and garlic. Cook and stir until beef is cooked through and lightly browned, about 5 minutes. Add ketchup, water and taco seasoning. Mix well and cook until mixture is hot and bubbly. Remove from heat.

To assemble bowlritos, equally divide hot rice mixture among 4 serving bowls. Top with hot, spiced beef and toppings of your choice. Pictured: Rice, beef, corn, black beans, salsa, guacamole, sour cream and cilantro. YUM!

Makes 4 servings

Per serving (rice and beef mixture only): 352 calories, 9.4 g total fat (3.9 g saturated fat), 34 g protein, 31 g carbohydrate (3.2 g fiber, 5 g sugars), 95 mg cholesterol, 408 mg sodium

SCAN FOR VIDEO!

Una fiesta MEXICANA!

YUM
Tastes delicious with ground chicken instead of beef.

YUMMER!
Top the rice and beef with Grilled Corn Salsa, page 210.

Better-Than-Takeout
Beef & Broccoli Stir-Fry

Why bother with takeout when Chinese food's so easy to make at home? My healthy rendition combines marinated beef with lightly steamed broccoli and a lip-smacking sauce for a fast and flavorful dinner.

Marinade

1 tbsp reduced-sodium soy sauce*

1 tbsp hoisin sauce*

2 tsp grated fresh gingerroot

1 tsp minced garlic

1 tsp cornstarch

1 lb (454 g) sirloin or flank steak, thinly sliced against the grain

Sauce

½ cup reduced-sodium beef broth

2 tbsp hoisin sauce

1 tbsp reduced-sodium soy sauce

2 tsp grated fresh gingerroot

2 tsp cornstarch

1 tsp minced garlic

1 tsp dark sesame oil

Pinch crushed red pepper flakes

1 tbsp peanut oil

4 cups broccoli florets

¼ cup chopped green onions (with white parts)

Toasted sesame seeds for garnish (optional)

In a medium bowl, whisk together all marinade ingredients until well blended. Add beef and toss to coat evenly with marinade. Let beef stand at room temperature for 20 minutes while you prepare the sauce and chop the broccoli.

Whisk together all sauce ingredients in a small bowl or measuring cup and set aside until ready to use. Heat peanut oil in a non-stick wok or skillet over medium-high heat. Add beef. Cook and stir until lightly browned, about 3 to 4 minutes. Remove beef from wok and keep warm. Add broccoli and ½ cup water to wok. Cook and stir until broccoli is tender-crisp, about 4 minutes, or cooked to your liking. (The water helps steam the broccoli, which is good! If your wok has a lid, use it!) Return beef to wok, stir in the onions and make a well in the center. Add sauce. Let it bubble a bit, then give everything a good stir and cook until sauce has thickened. Top with toasted sesame seeds before serving, if using.

Makes 4 servings

Per serving: 266 calories, 9.7 g total fat (2.5 saturated fat), 29 g protein, 16 g carbohydrate (3 g fiber, 6 g sugars), 39 mg cholesterol, 588 mg sodium

* For gluten-free, use Tamari soy sauce and GF hoisin sauce.

The takeout version of beef and broccoli is typically made with oyster sauce and Shaoxing wine (made from rice), but since I've made it my mission to use only common, easy-to-find ingredients in all of my recipes, I've switched to the more familiar hoisin sauce and ditched the wine. Still delicious!

SCAN FOR VIDEO!

SURE TO CAUSE A "*stir*"

YUM
If broccoli's not your thing, try sugar snap peas!

YUMMER!
Add color and crunch with a thinly sliced red bell pepper. Throw in some chopped fresh basil before serving. Delish!

Grilled Beef Tenderloin Steaks
with Lemon-Balsamic Barbecue Sauce

I've labeled this special-occasion recipe "Splurge-Worthy" not because it's loaded with fat or sodium or calories, but because it's expensive. For an occasional treat and for those who love meat, this tenderloin's flavor just can't be beat!

Barbecue Sauce

½ cup ketchup

2 tbsp freshly squeezed lemon juice

2 tbsp molasses

2 tbsp minced shallots

1 tbsp balsamic vinegar

1¼ tsp chili powder

1 tsp minced garlic

1 tsp grated lemon zest

1 tsp Dijon mustard

½ tsp each ground cumin and paprika

¼ tsp freshly ground black pepper

4 beef tenderloin steaks (about 6 oz/170 g each; see Kitchen Whizdom)

Sea salt and freshly ground black pepper

Combine all sauce ingredients in a small pot and bring to a gentle boil over medium-high heat. Reduce heat to low, cover and simmer for 2 minutes. Remove from heat and let cool before using.

Preheat grill to medium-high heat and lightly oil grill racks. Sprinkle steaks lightly on both sides with salt and pepper. Grill steaks for 4 to 5 minutes per side (with lid down), or until cooked to your desired degree of doneness. Exact cooking time will depend on thickness of steaks. Slather (and I mean SLATHER) the steaks with sauce during the last minute or two of cooking time. Let steaks rest for a couple of minutes before serving. Enjoy!

Note: Be careful not to ruin the steaks by overcooking them! Remember how much they cost? Enough said.

Makes 4 servings

Per serving: 300 calories, 10.3 g total fat (3.8 g saturated fat), 37 g protein, 13 g carbohydrate (0.5 g fiber, 9.8 g sugars), 101 mg cholesterol, 344 mg sodium

As someone who eats very little meat, when I do indulge, it better be great! I've been besieged by requests for this recipe, described by friends as "that amazing beef tenderloin you make." For even more flavor, I'll often rub the raw steaks with Montreal Steak Seasoning (instead of salt and pepper) before grilling. And I almost always add a hint of rosemary (not too much!) to the sauce. Choose any cut of steak you like, slather it with this sauce before serving and wait for the compliments. I'll *steak* my reputation on it!

SCAN FOR VIDEO!

SPLURGE-WORTHY

Wickedly Delicious

Totally Worth It!

YUM
This sauce tastes
great on grilled
pork loin chops!

YUMMER!
Add ½ tsp dried rosemary
and/or a pinch of cayenne
pepper to spice up the sauce.

Burger for a Better Planet
~ a.k.a The Blended Burger ~

Creating a mouthwatering burger that's healthier and more sustainable for the planet is the purpose behind the popular Blended Burger Project that's sweeping North America. Boost a burger's flavor, reduce calories and add nutrition by blending ground beef with earthy mushrooms? Sign me up!

8 oz (227 g) cremini mushrooms

2 tsp olive oil

⅓ cup minced onions

1¼ lbs (567 g) extra-lean ground beef

2 tbsp minced fresh parsley

2 tsp Burger Seasoning
(see recipe, page 189)

Barbecue sauce for basting
burgers (optional)

Toppings

Sliced tomatoes

Sliced pickles

Lettuce

Cheddar cheese slices

Guacamole

Or your favorite condiments

Place mushrooms in the bowl of a food processor and pulse on and off until mushrooms are finely chopped but not powdery.

Heat olive oil in a 10-inch, non-stick skillet over medium-high heat. Add mushrooms and onions. Cook and stir until mushrooms are tender and start to brown a bit, about 5 minutes. They should appear dry and crumbly, not wet. Remove from heat and let cool.

In a large bowl, combine beef, mushrooms, parsley and burger seasoning. Mix using your hands until all ingredients are well blended. Shape mixture into 4 patties. Cover with plastic wrap and refrigerate for 1 hour.

Preheat grill to medium-high heat and lightly oil grill racks. Grill burgers for about 5 minutes per side, or until cooked to your desired degree of doneness. During the last minute of cooking time, baste with barbecue sauce, if using. Serve immediately with buns or without, topped with your favorite burger garnishes.

Makes 4 burgers

Per burger (patty only): 218 calories, 9.4 g total fat (3.4 g saturated fat), 29 g protein, 4.5 g carbohydrate (0.8 g fiber, 1.8 g sugars), 78 mg cholesterol, 179 mg sodium

A healthy, delicious concept created by the Mushroom Council—yup, there is actually a council dedicated to mushrooms!—a blended burger combines juicy beef with meaty, minced mushrooms in an effort to reduce beef consumption without sacrificing flavor. You can apply this concept to tacos, chili, sloppy joes, hamburgers, meatloaf, meat sauce, etc. Start with a ratio of 25% mushroom to 75% beef and go from there. I love this idea and encourage you to visit www.blenditarian.com to learn more!

SCAN FOR VIDEO!

Juicy

Healthy

Extra Tasty!

YUM
Don't feel like making my homemade seasoning blend? No worries! Use whatever spices you prefer.

YUMMER!
Serve these burgers open-faced, topped with sliced tomatoes and guacamole!

PAPRIKA

GARLIC POWDER

ONION POWDER

BROWN SUGAR

CUMIN

MUSTARD POWDER

SEA SALT

BLACK PEPPER

CAYENNE PEPPER

SCAN FOR VIDEO!

MAKE YOUR OWN

Burger Seasoning

GF · DF · V

Use 2 to 3 tsp per pound of *ground meat.*

2 tbsp paprika
2 tsp brown sugar
  or coconut sugar
1½ tsp sea salt
1 tsp freshly ground
  black pepper
1 tsp ground cumin
1 tsp garlic powder
1 tsp onion powder
½ tsp mustard powder
¼ tsp cayenne pepper

Combine all ingredients in a small jar. Mix well.
Seal and store in your spice drawer for up to 3 months.

Makes about ⅓ cup seasoning

Per serving (1 tsp): 8 calories, 0.2 g total fat (0 g saturated fat)
0.3 g protein, 1.4 g carbohydrate (0.5 g fiber, 0.4 g sugars)
0 mg cholesterol, 215 mg sodium

Cranberry-Balsamic Roasted Pork Tenderloin
❧ with Orange & Rosemary ❧

(GF) (DF)

Easy enough for weekdays, fancy enough for company! This delectable roasted pork tenderloin with fresh cranberries cooks in a slightly tart, slightly sweet, totally scrumptious sauce featuring balsamic vinegar, maple syrup and a hint of orange and rosemary.

¼ cup balsamic vinegar

¼ cup freshly squeezed orange juice

3 tbsp grainy Dijon mustard

2 tbsp pure maple syrup

1 tbsp olive oil

2 tsp minced fresh rosemary, or ¾ tsp dried

2 tsp minced garlic

1 tsp grated orange zest
(see Kitchen Whizdom)

½ tsp each sea salt and freshly ground black pepper

2 large pork tenderloins (about 2½ to 3 lbs/1.1 to 1.4 kg)

¾ cup fresh or frozen cranberries (not dried)

Makes 6 servings

Per serving: 293 calories, 9.2 g total fat (2.7 g saturated fat), 40 g protein, 10 g carbohydrate (0.7 g fiber, 7 g sugars), 112 mg cholesterol, 441 mg sodium

Preheat oven to 400°F. In a small bowl or measuring cup, whisk together vinegar, orange juice, mustard, maple syrup, olive oil, rosemary, garlic, orange zest, salt and pepper.

In a glass or ceramic baking dish, arrange pork tenderloins side by side, but not touching. Pour sauce evenly over pork. Turn pork several times to make sure it's evenly coated with sauce. Sprinkle cranberries over pork.

Roast, uncovered, in preheated oven for 20 minutes. Carefully remove baking dish from oven and baste pork generously with sauce. Return pork to oven and roast for an additional 5 to 10 minutes, depending on size and thickness of pork. It's okay for pork to have a hint of pink in the center.

Let pork rest for 5 minutes before slicing. Slice into ½-inch-thick pieces and arrange on a serving platter. Give the sauce and berries a quick stir, then spoon over pork. Serve hot.

Add "zest" to your cooking with grated orange, lemon or lime peel! Be sure to wash your fruit before zesting and avoid grating the bitter white pith underneath the brightly colored outer layer. I know it sounds obvious, but if a recipe calls for both juice and zest (many of mine do!), make sure you zest first! It's frustrating and nearly impossible to zest squished lemon or lime halves. Finally, citrus zest freezes well! Zest your fruit with a Microplane, spoon the zest into a baggie and store it in the freezer.

SCAN FOR VIDEO!

YUM
Try fresh thyme
instead of rosemary.

YUMMER!
Add 12 peeled pearl onions
when you add the cranberries.

SCENT-
sational!

Beef & Italian Sausage Bolognese
a.k.a Presto Pasta Sauce

When you're craving pasta but don't feel like waiting for a slow-simmered sauce, this speedy, shortcut Bolognese with beef, sausage and veggies is the answer!

2 tsp olive oil

1¼ lbs (567 g) extra-lean ground beef

8 oz (227 g) mild or hot Italian sausage, casings removed

1 cup chopped onions

1 tsp minced garlic

2 cups chopped or sliced mushrooms

1 cup diced zucchini

2 jars (25 oz/700 mL each) your favorite marinara sauce (see Kitchen Whizdom)

1 tsp dried oregano, basil or Italian seasoning

¼ tsp freshly ground black pepper

Heat olive oil in a large soup pot over medium-high heat. Add beef, sausage, onions and garlic. Cook and stir until beef and sausage are no longer pink, breaking up any large chunks of meat as they cook. Drain and discard excess fat, if necessary.

Add mushrooms and zucchini. Cook and stir for 4 to 5 more minutes, until vegetables are tender. Add sauce, oregano and pepper. Bring mixture to a boil. Reduce heat to low, cover and simmer for 15 minutes. (This would be a good time to cook your pasta!) Serve over hot cooked pasta.

Makes about 8 cups sauce

Per cup: 277 calories, 10 g total fat (3.3 g saturated fat), 24 g protein, 22 g carbohydrate (6.7 g fiber, 9 g sugars), 62 mg cholesterol, 518 mg sodium

When you don't have the time or energy to whip up a batch of homemade pasta sauce, jarred or bottled sauces can help you get dinner on the table lickety-split. Be sure to compare the sodium content when choosing store-bought sauces, since it can range from 250 mg all the way up to 750 mg per half-cup serving! And who eats just half a cup? I mean, really. Not me, that's for sure! Next, check the sugar content, which also varies dramatically. Finally, it never hurts to choose a sauce that includes extra veggies in the recipe!

SCAN FOR VIDEO!

YUM
Ground chicken or turkey
can be used instead of beef.

YUMMER!
Try this meat sauce
in lasagna recipes!

TRY IT WITH QUINOA SPAGHETTI!!

Beef & Quinoa Meatloaf
✥ with Barbecue Sauce & Parmesan ✥

GF*

After modifying my mom's famous cabbage roll recipe by swapping cooked quinoa for plain white rice in the meat filling, it dawned on me that this healthier combo would make a marvelous meatloaf!

2 lbs (907 g) extra-lean ground beef

1 cup cooked quinoa

⅓ cup freshly grated Parmesan cheese

½ cup barbecue sauce, divided*

1 egg

¼ cup chopped fresh parsley

¼ cup grated or finely minced onions

2 tsp minced garlic

1 tsp dried basil

½ tsp freshly ground black pepper

* Double-check that your barbecue sauce is gluten-free if that's important to you.

Preheat oven to 350°F. Spray a broiler pan with cooking spray or lightly oil. Line bottom of pan with foil for easier clean up.

In a large bowl, combine beef, quinoa, Parmesan, ¼ cup barbecue sauce, egg, parsley, onions, garlic, basil and pepper. Mix well using your hands. Form mixture into an 8 x 4-inch loaf on prepared pan. Slather top and sides of loaf with remaining ¼ cup barbecue sauce.

Bake in preheated oven (uncovered) for about 1 hour and 20 minutes, or until meatloaf is cooked through.

Let meatloaf stand for 10 minutes before serving for easier slicing.

Makes 8 servings

Per serving: 256 calories, 11 g total fat (4.6 g saturated fat), 25 g protein, 11 g carbohydrate (1.2 g fiber, 5 g sugars), 97 mg cholesterol, 299 mg sodium

I prefer cooking meatloaf *on* a broiler pan versus *in* a loaf pan. Cooking a free-form loaf on a broiler pan allows the fat to drip away, plus the exposure to air helps form a nice crusty exterior all around the loaf, not just on the top. Standard loaf pans create soggy sides and bottoms, in my humble opinion. What's to loaf about that?

SCAN FOR VIDEO!

YUM
Use mild or spicy barbecue sauce, depending on your family's tastes.

YUMMER!
Serve with steamed green beans and Squashed Potatoes, page 214.

Gluten-free
QUINOA
replaces
BREAD CRUMBS

Sweet & Savory
Asian Grilled Pork Kabobs

Fire up the BBQ and get grilling! These flavorful, marinated pork tenderloin kabobs soaked with hoisin sauce, ginger and garlic are a walk in the pork to make. Bonus: Skewering meat versus grilling it whole means it'll cook much faster, too.

Marinade

⅓ cup hoisin sauce*

2 tbsp freshly squeezed lime juice

1 tbsp liquid honey

1 tbsp reduced-sodium soy sauce*

1 tbsp grated fresh gingerroot

2 tsp minced garlic

2 tsp dark sesame oil

1 tsp grated lime zest

2½ to 3 lbs (1.1 to 1.4 kg) pork tenderloin, cut into 1½-inch cubes

8 metal or wooden skewers**

* For gluten-free, use GF hoisin sauce and Tamari soy sauce.

** If using wooden skewers, soak them in cold water for at least an hour before using to prevent burning.

In a small bowl or measuring cup, whisk together all marinade ingredients until well blended. Reserve ¼ cup marinade for basting kabobs. Pour remaining marinade over pork cubes in a large, heavy-duty, resealable plastic bag. Seal bag and turn several times to coat pork evenly with marinade. Refrigerate for 1 to 4 hours.

Preheat grill to medium-high heat. Thread pork cubes onto skewers and discard marinade in bag. Lightly oil grill racks. Grill kabobs for about 8 minutes total, turning every 2 minutes or so. Baste generously with reserved marinade during last minute of cooking time. Really soak 'em with sauce! Serve hot.

Makes 8 kabobs

Per kabob: 232 calories, 7 g total fat (2.1 g saturated fat), 33 g protein, 7.8 g carbohydrate (0 g fiber, 5 g sugars), 90 mg cholesterol, 306 mg sodium

SCAN FOR VIDEO!

Delish-
KABOBS!

YUM
Try this marinade on
chicken thighs and drumsticks
or salmon fillets.

YUMMER!
Add a teaspoon or two of Sriracha
hot sauce to the marinade. Spicy!

Simple Sunday Pot Roast
with Potatoes, Carrots & Zesty Gravy

GF* DF

When I was a kid, our Sunday pot roast (cooked low and slow) was a welcome Podleski household tradition. The tender, fall-apart beef was impossible to resist, especially when paired with roasted potatoes and carrots and lightly drizzled with gravy.

1 boneless beef blade, cross-rib or chuck roast (3½ lbs/1.6 kg)

Sea salt and freshly ground black pepper

1 tbsp olive oil

1 large onion, cut into wedges

Sauce

1½ cups reduced-sodium beef broth

½ cup barbecue sauce*

2 tsp balsamic vinegar

2 tsp Dijon mustard

2 tsp minced garlic

1 tsp dried thyme

1 tsp dried rosemary

½ tsp freshly ground black pepper

2 lbs (907 g) yellow flesh potatoes, unpeeled, cut into chunks

1 lb (454 g) large carrots, scrubbed and coarsely chopped

2 tsp cornstarch

* For gluten-free, use GF barbecue sauce.

Preheat oven to 300°F.

Sprinkle roast on all sides with salt and pepper. Heat olive oil in a large Dutch oven over medium-high heat. Add roast and brown on all sides. Remove pot from heat and scatter onions around roast. Whisk together all sauce ingredients and pour over roast. Cover tightly and roast in preheated oven for 2 hours.

Carefully remove roast from oven and add potatoes and carrots to pot. Return to oven and roast for 90 more minutes, or until roast and vegetables are very tender. Transfer roast and vegetables to a serving platter and keep warm. Return pot with sauce to stovetop and skim off any visible fat. Mix cornstarch with 1 tbsp water until smooth and add to sauce. Cook and stir over medium-high heat until sauce is bubbly and gravy-like, about 1 minute.

Slice beef thinly and drizzle with gravy. Serve immediately.

Makes 8 servings

Per serving: 432 calories, 13.5 g total fat (5.2 g saturated fat), 39 g protein, 36 g carbohydrate (4.7 g fiber, 9 g sugars), 120 mg cholesterol, 304 mg sodium

The exact roasting time will vary based on the size of your roast, the accuracy of your oven temperature and whether or not you peeked during cooking. The key is "low and slow" so DO NOT crank up the heat. Yes, it smells divine. Yes, you're hungry. No, you don't want dry, chewy beef!

SCAN FOR VIDEO!

YUM
For a milder sauce, increase beef broth to 1¾ cups and reduce barbecue sauce to ¼ cup.

YUMMER!
I love this pot roast made with sweet potatoes instead of regular potatoes. Since they cook faster, cut the chunks a little larger.

Honey Mustard & Apple Cider
Saucy Skillet Pork Loin Chops

GF **DF**

A mild-tasting recipe that's perfect for a cool fall evening, these simple yet scrumptious pork chops smothered in savory onions and sweet-tart apples are a weeknight wonder!

1¼ cups apple cider, divided

3 tbsp honey mustard*

1 tbsp freshly squeezed lemon juice

2 tsp cornstarch

¼ tsp each sea salt and freshly ground
   black pepper + more for sprinkling
   over pork chops

4 thick pork loin chops
   (about 6 oz/170 g each)

1 tbsp olive oil

1 medium onion, sliced or chopped

2 tsp minced fresh thyme, or ¾ tsp dried

1 tsp minced garlic

1 large Gala apple, unpeeled, thinly sliced

* Please don't substitute Dijon for the honey mustard, as it will totally overpower the sauce.

Makes 4 servings

Per serving: 341 calories, 12.9 g total fat (4 g saturated fat), 34 g protein, 19 g carbohydrate (1.8 g fiber, 15 g sugars), 96 mg cholesterol, 272 mg sodium

In a large measuring cup, whisk together 1 cup apple cider, honey mustard, lemon juice, cornstarch, salt and pepper. Set sauce aside until ready to use.

Lightly sprinkle both sides of pork chops with salt and pepper. Heat olive oil in a deep, 10-inch, non-stick skillet over medium-high heat. Add pork chops and cook until browned on both sides, about 2 minutes per side. Reduce heat to low, cover and cook for about 10 minutes, turning once, until pork is almost cooked through and just slightly pink in the center.

Remove pork from skillet and keep warm. Do not drain pan juices. Return skillet to stovetop and increase heat to medium. Add onions and cook slowly until tender and beginning to caramelize, about 5 minutes. Stir in thyme and garlic and cook for 30 more seconds. Add apples and remaining ¼ cup apple cider. Mix well and continue to cook and stir for 2 minutes.

Add reserved sauce and cook until sauce is bubbly. Reduce heat to low, cover and simmer for 5 minutes or until apples are almost tender. Return pork to skillet, spoon sauce over pork, cover and simmer until pork is cooked through, about 5 more minutes, depending on thickness of pork.

Serve pork with apple and onion mixture spooned over top or (my preferred method) slice pork chops very thinly and return slices to skillet. Stir until slices are coated with sauce.

SCAN FOR VIDEO!

Lick
YOUR CHOPS!

YUM
Serve with a brown and wild
rice blend and a green veggie,
such as peas or broccoli.

YUMMER!
For a creamy sauce, remove pork chops from
skillet before serving and stir 3 tbsp whipping
cream into the apple and onion mixture.

CHAPTER 8

Side
WAYS

Simply scrumptious side dishes!

YUM & YUMMER

Maple-Balsamic Roasted Brussels Sprouts
with Toasted Almonds & Pomegranate

GF DF V

**Forget those boiled, soggy, unappealing Brussels sprouts of your childhood.
These easy-to-prepare, somewhat addictive sprouts are roasted to caramelized perfection,
making them a sensational side dish!**

2 lbs (907 g) Brussels sprouts

2 tbsp olive oil

2 tbsp balsamic vinegar

2 tbsp pure maple syrup

1 tbsp freshly squeezed lemon juice

1 tsp Dijon mustard

**Sea salt and freshly ground
black pepper to taste**

**¼ cup sliced or slivered almonds,
lightly toasted (see Kitchen Whizdom)**

¼ cup pomegranate seeds

Preheat oven to 400°F. Line a large, rimmed baking sheet with parchment paper and set aside. Trim the stem ends and remove any sad-looking outer leaves from the Brussels sprouts, then cut large sprouts in half lengthwise. You can leave the smaller sprouts whole. Place the Brussels sprouts in a large bowl.

In a small bowl or measuring cup, whisk together oil, vinegar, maple syrup, lemon juice, mustard and several grinds of salt and pepper. Pour dressing over Brussels sprouts and toss well, ensuring each sprout is coated with dressing. Spread Brussels sprouts evenly on prepared baking sheet in a single layer. Drizzle any extra dressing from bowl over sprouts. Get every last drop.

Roast, uncovered, for 10 minutes. Give Brussels sprouts a gentle stir, then continue to roast for about 15 more minutes, or until sprouts are tender and caramelized (or cooked to your liking).

Transfer roasted Brussels sprouts to a serving bowl and stir in almonds and pomegranate seeds. Serve immediately.

Makes 6 servings

Per serving: 154 calories, 7 g total fat (1 g saturated fat), 6 g protein, 21 g carbohydrate (7 g fiber, 9 g sugars), 0 mg cholesterol, 238 mg sodium

Nuts are tasty right outta their shells, but they're even better when toasted. The best news: Toasting only takes a few minutes! Just pour the nuts (almonds, in this case) into a small, dry skillet and place it over medium heat. Shake the skillet often (or stir) until nuts become fragrant and golden brown. This should take no more than 5 minutes. Transfer them to a small plate to cool before using.

SCAN FOR
VIDEO!

Ridiculously easy, surprisingly tasty!

Curried Coconut Rice
~ with Grilled Pineapple ~

GF DF V

Coconut and pineapple make a perfect pair—like chips and salsa, bacon and eggs, wine and cheese, Cam and Mitch. Fragrant and fantastically flavored, this jazzed up jasmine rice dish is slightly sticky and slightly sweet.

1 can (14 oz/398 mL) coconut milk (regular, not light)

2 tsp coconut oil or olive oil

1 cup diced onions

1½ cups uncooked jasmine or basmati rice

1 tsp grated fresh gingerroot

½ tsp curry powder

½ tsp sea salt

1 cup diced grilled pineapple (see Kitchen Whizdom)

2 to 3 tbsp minced fresh cilantro

Pour coconut milk into a large measuring cup and add water to make 3 cups. Set aside.

Heat coconut oil in a medium pot over medium heat. Add onions and cook until onions are tender, about 3 minutes, stirring often.

Add rice, gingerroot and curry. Cook and stir for 1 minute. Stir in coconut milk mixture and salt. Bring to a gentle boil. Reduce heat to low, cover and simmer until liquid is absorbed and rice is tender, about 12 minutes. (Check suggested cooking time on rice packaging.)

Remove rice from heat and let stand, covered, for 10 minutes. Fluff rice and add diced pineapple and cilantro. Serve hot.

Makes 6 servings

Per serving: 287 calories, 11 g total fat (9.6 g saturated fat), 4.3 g protein, 41 g carbohydrate (1.3 g fiber, 5.2 g sugars), 0 mg cholesterol, 200 mg sodium

Most fruits are too fragile for grilling but pineapple's an exception. Plus, grilling it makes it exceptionally flavorful! I usually buy a pre-cored pineapple, which often costs the same as the whole, unpeeled fruit. No-brainer time-saver! Preheat your grill to medium-high heat. Slice the pineapple into ¾-inch-thick rings. Brush the rings lightly with olive oil (or melted butter) on both sides. Grill for about 3 to 4 minutes per side, until pineapple is heated through and is sporting some nice grill marks. Done! Your pineapple is now a fineapple and you can dice it up for this recipe or serve it as a side dish to anything else you're grilling.

SCAN FOR VIDEO!

You'll PINE FOR GRILLED *pineapple!*

YUM
Not a fan of cilantro?
Use parsley instead.

YUMMER!
Cuckoo for coconut?
Garnish with toasted
coconut flakes
before serving.

Roasted Fall Vegetables

 with Herbs

GF **DF** **V**

Eat 'em when it's autumn! This marvelous medley of colorful vegetables is sure to be a hit at any seasonal feast. Roasting brings out the best in veggies, making them naturally sweeter and tastier.

12 mini red, white or purple
  potatoes, unpeeled, halved
  (see Kitchen Whizdom)

6 medium carrots, peeled and cut
  into 1-inch pieces

1 small fennel bulb, trimmed
  and cut into 1-inch slices
  (see Kitchen Whizdom)

1 large or two medium parsnips,
  peeled and cut into 1-inch pieces

1 large red onion, cut into 8 wedges

½ small butternut squash, peeled
  and cut into 1-inch pieces

3 tbsp olive oil

1 tsp balsamic vinegar

½ tsp each sea salt and freshly
  ground black pepper

1 tbsp minced fresh rosemary,
  or 1 tsp dried

1 tbsp minced fresh thyme,
  or 1 tsp dried

Preheat oven to 400°F.

Place potatoes, carrots, fennel, parsnips, onion wedges and squash in a very large mixing bowl. In a small bowl, whisk together olive oil, vinegar, salt and pepper. Pour over vegetables. Toss vegetables until evenly coated with oil mixture. (Using your hands works well, too!) Sprinkle herbs over vegetables and toss again.

Spread vegetables evenly on a very large, non-stick, rimmed baking sheet or on two smaller baking sheets. Be careful not to crowd the vegetables or they will steam, not roast! As much as possible, they should be in a single layer.

Roast vegetables, uncovered, for 20 minutes. Remove from oven and give veggies a stir. Return to oven, rotating pans if necessary, and bake for 15 to 25 more minutes, depending on thickness of vegetables. Be careful not to burn them! Serve hot.

Makes 8 servings

Per serving: 185 calories, 5.8 g total fat (0.8 g saturated fat), 3.5 g protein, 33 g carbohydrate (6.5 g fiber, 7 g sugars), 0 mg cholesterol, 194 mg sodium

Look for small bags of tiny colored potatoes in the produce section of your grocery store. They usually contain a mix of white, red and purple potatoes and work very well in this recipe. If you can't find mini potatoes, you can buy fingerling potatoes or regular potatoes and cut them into 1-inch cubes. The key is to cut all of the vegetables into 1-inch pieces (approximately) to ensure even roasting. Otherwise, your squash and onions will be tender while your carrots and potatoes are still rock hard. To trim fennel, cut off and discard stalks and ½ inch off bottom of bulb. Cut bulb in half. Place flat side down on cutting board. Cut each fennel half into 1-inch slices.

 SCAN FOR VIDEO!

YUM
Golden beets would make a fabulous addition to this recipe!

YUMMER!
Use leftover roasted veggies in a healthy grain bowl (see recipe, page 100).

Stop and smell the rosemary!

Crisp & Colorful
Grilled Corn Salsa

 GF DF V

Is it salsa? Or is it salad? A salsalad? You decide! One thing's for certain: It's outrageously delicious! Serve with grilled anything: beef, pork, chicken, fish or portobello mushrooms.

6 medium cobs fresh corn, shucked

1½ cups quartered grape tomatoes

⅓ cup very thinly sliced red onions

3 tbsp minced fresh cilantro

1 jalapeño pepper, minced

2 tbsp olive oil

2 tbsp freshly squeezed lime juice

¼ tsp each ground cumin and
   chili powder

¼ tsp sea salt

Preheat grill to medium-high heat. Brush grill (or corn) lightly with oil. Place corn directly on the grill. Make sure the cobs are resting between the grates to avoid a cob-rolling situation. Close lid. Grill corn until char marks appear and corn is tender, rotating corn every 2 to 3 minutes. Total cooking time will be 10 to 12 minutes. (Note: There are a dozen ways to grill corn, but this technique is simpler and faster when corn is being used in salsa or salad.)

Remove corn from heat. When corn is cool enough to handle, slice the kernels off the cob and place them in a medium bowl. Add all remaining ingredients and mix well. Serve immediately or cover and refrigerate until serving time.

Makes about 5 cups salsa

Per serving (½ cup): 81 calories, 3.5 g total fat (0.4 g saturated fat), 2.2 g protein, 12 g carbohydrate (1.7 g fiber, 2.8 g sugars), 0 mg cholesterol, 62 mg sodium

SCAN FOR VIDEO!

YUM
Looks gorgeous and tastes amazing with multi-colored grape tomatoes (pictured).

YUMMER!
Add grilled shrimp, diced avocados and some black beans for a sensational summertime meal.

Do the salsa!

Melon Mojito Salsa

GF **DF** **V**

This refreshing, delicious salsa combines three types of juicy melons with tangy lime and fresh mint for a summery flavor explosion! It requires a bit of chopping, but it's worth it. Adds a splash of color and just the right amount of zing to any main dish.

1½ cups each diced watermelon, cantaloupe and honeydew melon (see Kitchen Whizdom)

1 cup peeled, diced English cucumbers

¼ cup finely minced red onions (or use green onions with white parts)

1 small jalapeño pepper, minced

2 to 3 tbsp minced fresh mint (or cilantro, or a bit of both!)

2 tbsp freshly squeezed lime juice

½ tsp grated lime zest

¼ tsp each sea salt and freshly ground black pepper

In a large bowl, combine watermelon, cantaloupe, honeydew, cucumbers, onions and jalapeño. Mix gently.

Add mint, lime juice and zest, salt and pepper and toss gently.

Cover and refrigerate until serving time.

Makes about 5½ cups salsa

Per serving (½ cup): 26 calories, 0.2 g total fat (0 g saturated fat), 0.6 g protein, 6.2 g carbohydrate (0.7 g fiber, 5.2 g sugars), 0 mg cholesterol, 57 mg sodium

Since watermelon is so, well, watery…spread out the diced pieces on a couple sheets of paper towels to dry them slightly before mixing with the other ingredients. To save time, look for a tray of pre-cut melon chunks in the produce section of your grocery store. The three melons in this recipe are often packaged together. Then you'll simply need to dice them into smaller pieces, leaving you plenty of time to make a REAL mojito. ☺

SCAN FOR VIDEO!

Like a MOJITO – without the HANGOVER!

YUM
Dislike cantaloupe? No problem!
Use diced mango.

YUMMER!
Tastes GREAT with
grilled fish or shrimp!

Roasted Garlic Cauliflower Mash (GF)

1 large head cauliflower, cut into florets

1 small onion, coarsely chopped

2 tbsp + ½ tsp olive oil

3 large cloves garlic, peeled, left whole

½ cup extra-smooth ricotta cheese

½ tsp sea salt

¼ tsp freshly ground black pepper

On a large, non-stick baking sheet, toss florets and onion with 2 tbsp olive oil. Put garlic cloves in a small piece of foil and drizzle with ½ tsp olive oil. Seal foil and place on pan with cauliflower. Roast for 15 minutes at 400°F. Stir or flip pieces. Roast for 15 more minutes until tender. Transfer veggies and garlic to a food processor. Add ricotta, salt and pepper. Whirl until desired consistency is reached, scraping down bowl as needed.

Makes 5 servings

(GF) SQUASHED potatoes

2 lbs (907 g) Yukon Gold potatoes, peeled and cut into large chunks

½ small butternut squash, peeled and cut into large chunks

½ cup freshly grated Parmesan cheese

½ cup 5% sour cream

½ tsp sea salt

¼ tsp freshly ground black pepper

Dash nutmeg

Minced fresh chives for garnish (optional)

In a large pot, boil potatoes and squash until tender. Drain and return to pot. Sprinkle Parmesan over vegetables, cover with lid and let stand 1 minute. Add sour cream, salt, pepper and nutmeg. Beat with a handheld mixer until smooth.

Makes 8 servings

Whip it GOOD!

See page 285 for Nutritional Info.

GF DF V

MAPLE-BUTTER
Sweet Potatoes

3 lbs (1.4 kg) sweet potatoes
(3 large or 5 medium)

2 tbsp butter or vegan buttery spread

2 tbsp pure maple syrup

½ tsp sea salt

¼ tsp freshly ground black pepper

Pinch each ground cinnamon and nutmeg (optional)

Pierce potato skins 5 or 6 times with a fork. Place on baking sheet and bake at 400°F until tender. Cool slightly. Cut potatoes in half, scoop out flesh into bowl, discard skins. Add remaining ingredients to bowl and whip with handheld mixer until smooth.

Makes 6 servings

 SCAN FOR VIDEO!

Roasted Squash & Ricotta Stuffed Shells
⇝ with Alfredo Sauce ⇜

These creamy, decadently delicious stuffed pasta shells are the ultimate fall comfort food.

Squash/Filling

4 cups peeled, cubed butternut squash*

2 tsp olive oil

1 tsp dried sage

Pinch sea salt and freshly ground
   black pepper

1½ cups extra-smooth ricotta cheese

½ cup freshly grated Parmesan cheese

½ pkg frozen chopped spinach,
   thawed and squeezed dry
   (⅓ cup packed after drying)

1 egg

Pinch nutmeg or pumpkin pie spice

20 uncooked jumbo pasta shells

Sauce

2 tbsp butter

2 tsp minced garlic

1¼ cups 5% light cream

1 tbsp all-purpose flour

½ cup freshly grated Parmesan cheese

½ tsp grated lemon zest (important!)

Pinch sea salt and freshly ground
   black pepper

* For convenience, you could buy a 1-lb (454 g) package of fresh, ready-to-cook butternut squash cubes for this recipe. I always cut the cubes in half so they'll roast faster.

Preheat oven to 400°F. Line a small baking pan with parchment paper and set aside.

In a large bowl, combine squash, olive oil, sage, salt and pepper. Toss until squash is evenly coated with seasonings. Spread squash in a single layer on prepared pan. Roast for 20 minutes or until squash is tender. Stir once, halfway through cooking time. Let cool and mash well with a fork or potato masher.

While squash is roasting, make filling and cook shells. In a medium bowl, combine ricotta, Parmesan, spinach, egg, nutmeg and a pinch of salt and pepper. Mix well. Cover and refrigerate until ready to use. Cook shells according to package directions or until al dente. Rinse with cold water and drain well.

Add mashed squash to ricotta filling and mix well. Stuff each shell with about 2 tbsp of filling. Once all shells are stuffed, set them aside and quickly make the sauce. In a small pot, melt butter over medium heat. When frothy, add garlic. Cook and stir for 1 minute, or until garlic becomes golden. Whisk together cream and flour in a measuring cup until smooth with no lumps. Add to pot. Cook, whisking constantly, until mixture bubbles and begins to thicken. Add Parmesan, lemon zest, salt and pepper. Whisk until cheese is melted. Remove from heat.

Reduce oven temperature to 375°F. Spray a casserole dish with cooking spray or lightly oil. Spread ½ cup sauce over bottom of dish. Arrange shells over sauce. Drizzle remaining sauce evenly over shells. Cover loosely with foil and bake for 25 minutes. Uncover and bake for 10 more minutes. Cool slightly before serving.

Makes 20 stuffed shells

Per shell: 122 calories, 6 g total fat (3.4 g saturated fat), 6.3 g protein, 12.7 g carbohydrate (1.1 g fiber, 2.4 g sugars), 30 mg cholesterol, 185 mg sodium

SCAN FOR VIDEO!

YUM
Have a favorite brand of pre-made Alfredo sauce? Go ahead and use it in this recipe!

YUMMER!
Tastes extra-creamy and decadent when roasted, mashed sweet potatoes are used instead of squash.

Wickedly Delicious
SPLURGE-WORTHY
Totally Worth It!

Moroccan-Spiced Couscous
with Chickpeas & Almonds

A busy cook's best friend, couscous is ready in 5 minutes, making it a popular choice
for weeknight meals. Plus, you can jazz up couscous in so many flavorful ways!
This warmly spiced version with lots of texture and crunch is one of my faves.
I've labeled this a side dish but I've eaten it as a vegetarian main course many times.

- 2 tsp olive oil
- ¾ cup diced onions
- 1 tsp minced garlic
- 1 cup reduced-sodium vegetable broth
  or water
- ½ cup orange juice
- ½ tsp each ground cinnamon, cumin,
  coriander, ginger, curry powder
  and sea salt
- ¼ tsp freshly ground black pepper
- 1 cup whole wheat couscous
- 1 cup cooked chickpeas
- ¼ cup dried currants
- ⅓ cup sliced almonds (toasted is nice!)
- 2 tbsp minced fresh mint, cilantro
  or parsley

Heat olive oil in a medium pot over medium heat. Add onions and garlic. Cook and stir until onions begin to soften, about 3 minutes.

Add broth, orange juice and spices. Mix well and bring mixture to a boil. Reduce heat to low and stir in couscous, chickpeas and currants. Cook for 1 minute, then remove from heat. Let mixture stand, covered, for 5 minutes.

Give the couscous a good fluff, then stir in almonds and mint. Serve hot.

Makes 6 servings

Per serving: 221 calories, 5.6 g total fat (0.6 g saturated fat), 7.7 g protein, 37 g carbohydrate (5 g fiber, 8.6 g sugars), 0 mg cholesterol, 206 mg sodium

SCAN FOR VIDEO!

SPICE *up your* Life!

YUM
Need gluten-free? Look for gluten-free couscous in the health-food section of your grocery store.

YUMMER!
Stir in one cup of diced, roasted butternut squash or sweet potatoes before serving for a tasty vegetarian meal. Serves 4.

Roasted Cauliflower
⟿ with *Parmesan & Thyme* ⟾

Transform plain ol' cauliflower from drab to fab by roasting it with olive oil and thyme and topping it with Parmesan! You may never eat steamed or boiled cauliflower again once you taste what a little lovin' in the oven can do.

1 large head cauliflower

2 tbsp olive oil

1 to 2 tbsp minced fresh thyme

1 tbsp freshly squeezed lemon juice

1 tsp minced garlic

¼ tsp each sea salt and freshly ground black pepper

⅓ cup freshly grated Parmesan cheese

Preheat oven to 400°F. Cut the cauliflower into florets or slices or some of each (see photo). As long as your pieces are about the same thickness, the cauliflower will cook properly. Arrange cauliflower in a single layer on a large, non-stick, rimmed baking sheet.

In a small bowl, whisk together olive oil, thyme, lemon juice and garlic. Drizzle oil mixture over cauliflower florets and toss or stir to coat all sides. Using your hands works best! Sprinkle with salt and pepper.

Roast cauliflower for 15 minutes. Stir or flip pieces over and roast for 10 more minutes. Sprinkle cauliflower with Parmesan and roast until cheese is melted and cauliflower is tender when pierced with a fork, about 3 more minutes. Serve immediately.

Makes 6 servings

Per serving: 102 calories, 6.8 g total fat (1.7 g saturated fat), 5.1 g protein, 8.2 g carbohydrate (3.7 g fiber, 3.7 g sugars), 5 mg cholesterol, 239 mg sodium

For a vegan version, replace the Parmesan cheese with nutritional yeast. What is that, you ask? Nutritional yeast may not sound very appetizing, but it's actually quite tasty, so I recommend giving it a chance. Specifically, it's an inactive (meaning dead) form of the yeast strain known as *Saccharomyces cerevisiae* and it kinda looks like fish-food flakes. Okay…not really presenting my case very well here, am I? Let's try again. Ever tried "cheesy" kale chips? Yum, right? That's nutritional yeast in action! The yellow flakes have a nutty, savory, sorta creamy flavor, making them a good cheese substitute for vegans or for those who need dairy-free options. You'll find nutritional yeast in the health-food section of well-stocked ~~pet food~~ grocery stores or you can order it online.

SCAN FOR VIDEO!

Caramelized goodness!

YUM
Use half thyme
and half rosemary.

YUMMER!
Serve with your favorite
marinara sauce for dunking.

Roasted Acorn Squash
with Spiced Orange-Maple Butter

It's acorn-ucopia of flavors! Try this mouthwatering squash recipe paired with roasted turkey, pork tenderloin or as part of a vegetarian meal. It's so simple, yet so delicious!

1 medium to large acorn squash
(about 2½ lbs/1.1 kg)
2 tbsp butter, melted*
1 tbsp pure maple syrup
1 tsp garam masala spice blend
(see Kitchen Whizdom)
½ tsp grated orange zest
½ tsp sea salt

* Use a vegan buttery spread to make this recipe both vegan and dairy-free.

Preheat oven to 400°F. Line a large, rimmed baking sheet with parchment paper and set aside.

Wash and dry squash. Cut squash in half lengthwise from the stem to the bottom end. Scoop out and discard the seeds. Cut squash halves crosswise into ¾-inch-thick slices. You should end up with 10 to 12 slices in total. Place squash pieces on prepared pan in a single layer.

In a small bowl, whisk together butter, maple syrup, garam masala, orange zest and salt. Spoon or brush mixture evenly over both sides of squash pieces. Use every drop!

Roast squash for 15 minutes. Carefully remove pan from oven, flip pieces over and roast for 15 more minutes, until squash is tender. Serve immediately.

Makes 4 servings

Per serving: 155 calories, 5.8 g total fat (4 g saturated fat), 2 g protein, 27 g carbohydrate (3.7 g fiber, 3.3 g sugars), 15 mg cholesterol, 274 mg sodium

What is garam masala? It's a highly aromatic blend of roasted, ground spices commonly used in Indian cooking, including coriander, cumin, cinnamon, cloves, cardamom and black peppercorns. You really must try it! Look for garam masala in the regular spice aisle of your grocery store or at any gourmet food shop. Acorn squash skin is edible, however, some people don't like it. Hey, it's no skin off my back! Just peel off the skin after roasting.

SCAN FOR VIDEO!

ACORN
SQUASH
SKIN
is edible!

YUM
Try it with pumpkin pie
spice instead of garam masala.

YUMMER!
Sprinkle fresh pomegranate
seeds and minced, fresh parsley
on the squash before serving
(pictured).

Sesame-Hoisin Asparagus

Willing to try a new asparagus recipe? That's the spear-it! As you've likely figured out by now, roasting vegetables is my favorite way to prepare them. When it comes to asparagus, an Asian glaze is a tasty change from the standard roast-in-olive-oil-and-sea-salt-then-sprinkle-with-lemon-juice version. Try this recipe on asparagus skeptics who think the vegetable's too bitter.

1½ lbs (680 g) fresh asparagus
  (see Kitchen Whizdom)
2 tbsp hoisin sauce*
1 tbsp freshly squeezed lemon juice
2 tsp olive oil
1 tsp dark sesame oil
1 to 2 tbsp sesame seeds
Freshly ground black pepper to taste

* For gluten-free, use GF hoisin sauce.

Preheat oven to 425°F. Trim tough, woody ends off asparagus and spread them in a single layer on a large, non-stick, rimmed baking sheet. (Some people actually peel the bottom part of the spear. Yes, for real. I honestly can't be bothered!)

In a small bowl, whisk together hoisin sauce, lemon juice, olive oil and sesame oil. Pour mixture over asparagus. Using your hands (yeah, it's a little messy), rub glaze all over asparagus, then sprinkle with sesame seeds.

Roast for 10 to 12 minutes, until spears are tender and lightly browned. Exact roasting time will depend on thickness of asparagus. Be careful not to overcook them. Sad, soggy asparagus is no fun and no yum. Top with a grind or two of pepper and serve immediately.

Makes 6 servings

Per serving: 60 calories, 2.8 g total fat (0.4 g saturated fat), 3 g protein, 7.5 g carbohydrate (3 g fiber, 3.7 g sugars), 0 mg cholesterol, 89 mg sodium

Roasting asparagus is the easiest, tastiest way to prepare it. For the best flavor, buy and cook asparagus on the same day. Choose the freshest asparagus possible. How to tell if it's fresh? Look at the tips and stems. If the tips are tightly closed, the stems are firm (not limp) and the entire spear is a bright shade of green, you're good to go! Be careful when roasting the pencil-thin variety, since it dries out very quickly and is easier to overcook. In other words, don't browse Facebook or start a load of laundry while your asparagus is roasting.

SCAN FOR VIDEO!

Roast for the MOST flavor!

YUM
Try this recipe with fresh, trimmed green beans instead of asparagus.

YUMMER!
Spice up the glaze with a few drops of hot sauce or a pinch of cayenne pepper.

Coconut Oil Roasted Sweet Potatoes
with Chili-Lime Dipping Sauce

When you slice up a sweet potato, toss it in coconut oil and savory spices, then roast it at high heat, it becomes a sweet potatWHOA! A healthy snack or side dish, these highly addictive wedges taste great with chili-lime dipping sauce or plain ol' ketchup.

Dipping Sauce

1 cup thick 2% Greek yogurt

2 tbsp freshly squeezed lime juice

1 tsp liquid honey

½ tsp grated lime zest

¼ tsp chili powder

¼ tsp ground cumin

¼ tsp each sea salt and freshly
   ground black pepper

Wedges

4 medium sweet potatoes
   (about 2½ lbs/1.1 kg), unpeeled

2 tbsp coconut oil, melted
   (or olive oil)

1 tsp paprika

1 tsp dried oregano

1 tsp ground cumin

½ tsp each sea salt and freshly
   ground black pepper

Chopped green onions for garnish
   (optional)

In a small bowl, whisk together all sauce ingredients. Cover and refrigerate until serving time.

Preheat oven to 425°F. Line a large, rimmed baking sheet with parchment paper and set aside.

Wash potatoes and pat dry using paper towels. Slice into ½-inch-thick wedges. Place wedges in a large bowl and toss with coconut oil. Add paprika, oregano, cumin, salt and pepper. Toss again, making sure all wedges are well coated with oil and spices.

Spread wedges in a single layer on prepared pan. (If crowded, use two baking sheets.) Roast for 10 minutes. Carefully flip wedges over and continue to roast for 12 to 15 more minutes, or until potatoes are lightly browned and tender. Be careful not to burn them. Serve immediately topped with green onions, if using.

Makes 4 to 6 servings

Per serving (based on 6 servings, wedges only): 207 calories, 4.9 g total fat (0.7 g saturated fat), 3 g protein, 39 g carbohydrate (6.1 g fiber, 8 g sugars), 0 mg cholesterol, 283 mg sodium

Per 2-tbsp sauce: 32 calories, 0.6 g total fat (0.4 g saturated fat), 4 g protein, 4.3 g carbohydrate (0.4 g fiber, 1.4 g sugars), 3 mg cholesterol, 148 mg sodium

 SCAN FOR VIDEO!

Nutritionally, sweet potatoes are the GREATER TATER!

YUM
For a vegan dipping sauce, replace the Greek yogurt with 1 cup mashed, ripe avocado.

YUMMER!
Turn up the heat by adding a squeeze of Sriracha to the dipping sauce. You could also sub mayo for the yogurt.

CHAPTER 9

Sweets & TREATS

The carbs are on the table!

YUM & YUMMER

Grab & Go

Almond Butter Energy Bites

GF* DF* V

The perfect afternoon, after-workout or after-school snack, these blissful balls of yumminess take about 15 minutes to make and there's no baking involved. How sweet is that?

⅔ cup quick-cooking oats (not instant)*

⅓ cup unsweetened shredded coconut

⅓ cup mini semi-sweet chocolate chips*

2 tbsp flax meal (ground flaxseed)
   or ground chia seeds

1 cup natural almond butter

¼ cup pure maple syrup

1 tsp vanilla

* For gluten-free bites, make sure your oats are certified gluten-free. For dairy-free and vegan, use dairy-free chocolate chips, found in the health-food aisle of your grocery store. Chop up large chips so they're the size of minis, otherwise the balls will fall apart.

In a small bowl, combine oats, coconut, chocolate chips and flax meal. Mix well and set aside.

In a medium bowl, mix almond butter, maple syrup and vanilla until smooth. I use a wooden spoon for this. Add oat mixture and stir again until all ingredients are well blended. It'll look like raw cookie dough. Yum!

Using about 1 tbsp dough per energy bite, roll mixture into 20 balls using your hands. Wet hands occasionally to help prevent dough from sticking. Store in an airtight container in the fridge.

Makes 20 energy bites

Per bite: 120 calories, 8.4 g total fat (1.5 g saturated fat), 5.5 g protein, 10 g carbohydrate (2.1 g fiber, 5 g sugars), 1 mg cholesterol, 43 mg sodium

Since nut butters can often cost an almond a leg, I like making my own! Have you tried my recipe on page 258? You really must! I'm obsessed with nut butters and sunflower butter and have at least four jars on the go at any given time. I slather almond or cashew butter on a banana and eat it for breakfast, add peanut butter to my smoothies and eat sunflower butter by the spoonful when I need a quick snack. I'm in love with SunButter brand (for sunflower butter) and Nuts to You Nut Butter brand (Canada) for all nut butters. In the U.S., I'd highly recommend Justin's almond butter and peanut butter. Sooooo good!

SCAN FOR VIDEO!

YUM
Can't have nuts? Make this recipe with sunflower butter. Delicious!

YUMMER!
If you're a cinnamon lover, add ½ tsp ground cinnamon to the wet ingredients.

Love at first BITE! ♥

Banana Walnut Snack Cake
❧ with Chocolate Swirl ❧

If you're nuts about bananas, this simple and scrumptious snack cake is a must-bake recipe! It's the perfect way to use up your overripe bananas, plus your kitchen will smell heavenly while the cake is baking. Don't feel like making the chocolate swirl? No problem, just stir the chocolate chips into the batter.

1 cup whole wheat flour

1 cup all-purpose flour

2 tsp baking powder

1 tsp baking soda

1 tsp ground cinnamon

½ tsp sea salt

1½ cups mashed super-ripe
bananas

¾ cup plain 2% Greek yogurt

½ cup brown sugar (not packed)

2 eggs

¼ cup sunflower or safflower oil
(I use organic)

2 tsp vanilla

⅓ cup dark chocolate chips,
melted (see Kitchen Whizdom)

½ cup chopped walnuts

Preheat oven to 350°F. Spray a 9-inch square baking pan with cooking spray or lightly oil. Optional: Cover bottom of pan with parchment paper for easier cake removal.

In a medium bowl, combine both flours, baking powder, baking soda, cinnamon and salt. Mix well and set aside.

In a large bowl, whisk together bananas, yogurt, sugar, eggs, oil and vanilla until well blended. Add dry ingredients to wet ingredients and stir just until dry ingredients are moistened. Transfer ½ cup batter to a small bowl and add melted chocolate; mix well.

Fold walnuts into banana batter and spread batter evenly in prepared pan. Drop small dollops of chocolate batter over banana batter. Drag a knife through both batters in a zigzag pattern to swirl top.

Bake for 30 to 35 minutes, or until a wooden pick inserted in center of cake comes out clean. Cool on a wire rack. Tastes great served warm.

Makes 12 servings

Per serving: 257 calories, 11 g total fat (2.3 g saturated fat), 7 g protein, 34 g carbohydrate (3.3 g fiber, 13.5 g sugars), 32 mg cholesterol, 226 mg sodium

There are several ways to melt chocolate, just remember never to let a drop of water touch it, since that'll cause the chocolate to seize and become a clumpy, unusable mass. My microwave has a "melt chocolate" setting that works great! The key is to melt the chocolate SLOWLY over low heat, whether in your microwave or on the stovetop. Don't scorch it or burn it! On the stovetop, place chocolate in a metal or glass bowl that fits snugly over a pot of simmering water. Stir often until chocolate is shiny, smooth and completely melted.

SCAN FOR
VIDEO!

Bursting WITH banana flavor!

YUM

For muffins, stir unmelted chocolate chips into the batter and bake for about 22 minutes.

YUMMER!

Coconut lover? Add ½ cup unsweetened flaked coconut when you add the walnuts.

Fruit-Filled & Flavorful Blueberry Cornmeal Muffins

If I was allowed to eat only one type of muffin for the rest of my life, it would be these classic blueberry cornmeal muffins. Subtly sweet, light and lemony, bursting with blueberry goodness—in my opinion, there's *muffin* better!

1¼ cups all-purpose flour

¾ cup cornmeal (see Kitchen Whizdom)

2 tsp baking powder

½ tsp baking soda

½ tsp sea salt

1 can (14 oz/398 mL) cream-style corn

¼ cup sunflower or safflower oil
  (I use organic)

¼ cup liquid honey

1 egg

1 tbsp freshly squeezed lemon juice

Grated zest of 1 lemon

1 cup fresh blueberries

Preheat oven to 375°F. Spray a 12-cup muffin tin with cooking spray or lightly oil and set aside. (Or use paper liners.)

In a large bowl, whisk together flour, cornmeal, baking powder, baking soda and salt. Set aside.

In a medium bowl, whisk together corn, oil, honey, egg, lemon juice and zest. Add wet ingredients to dry ingredients and stir just until dry ingredients are moistened. Fold in blueberries. Do not overmix.

Evenly spoon batter into prepared cups and bake for about 20 minutes, or until a wooden pick inserted in center of muffin comes out clean (or with just a few moist crumbs). Transfer muffins to a wire rack to cool. Serve warm.

Makes 12 muffins

Per muffin: 160 calories, 5.6 g total fat (0.5 g saturated fat), 2.8 g protein, 26 g carbohydrate (1.8 g fiber, 8 g sugars), 16 mg cholesterol, 180 mg sodium

This recipe calls for cornmeal, not corn flour. What's the difference? Cornmeal is simply dried and ground corn with a grainy texture. It's made by grinding yellow, white or blue corn, though you'll mostly see the yellow-corn variety at your grocery store and that's what I use for this recipe. Corn flour is just finely ground (powdery) cornmeal and isn't interchangeable with cornmeal in most baking recipes. Most importantly, it won't provide the signature texture that makes these muffins a-maize-ing.

SCAN FOR VIDEO!

NOTHIN'
BEATS A
freshly baked
muffin!

No-Bake, No-Fail
Double Chocolate Mousse Cheesecake

This over-the-top dessert always draws rave reviews! I love that there's no baking involved and that guests literally squeal when they taste it. Make this cake your "once-a-year treat" for a special occasion.

Cake

1½ cups Oreo cookie crumbs*

¼ cup butter, melted

1½ cups heavy (whipping) cream

1 lb (454 g) semi-sweet chocolate

12 oz (340 g) light cream cheese**

¾ cup light brown sugar (not packed)

1 tsp vanilla

3 tbsp coffee liqueur (Kahlúa) or Irish cream liqueur (optional)

Garnishes

Whipped cream

Fresh raspberries or sliced strawberries

Chocolate drizzle

* You can make this recipe gluten-free by whirling gluten-free chocolate wafer cookies in your food processor and using them instead of the Oreo crumbs.

** Why use light cream cheese in an ultra-decadent cheesecake? I have no idea! It's kinda like ordering a diet Coke to go with your cheeseburger and fries, right? But I've always made it this way and it works perfectly, so if it ain't broke….

Spray bottom and sides of an 8-inch springform pan (or lightly oil). Cut a piece of parchment paper to fit bottom and line pan with parchment.

In a medium bowl, stir together crumbs and butter using a fork until all crumbs are moistened. Press mixture onto bottom (not sides) of springform pan. Really pack it down. Cover and refrigerate for 1 hour to set crust.

In a medium, deep metal or glass bowl (chilled if possible), whip the cream on medium speed of an electric mixer until stiff peaks form. Cover and chill until ready to use. Melt the chocolate (see Kitchen Whizdom, page 232) and let cool slightly before using.

In a large bowl, beat the cream cheese, sugar and vanilla on medium speed of electric mixer until well blended and perfectly smooth. Add liqueur, if using, and beat again. Add the cooled, melted chocolate and beat until well blended. Fold in the chilled whipped cream. Do not use the beater for this! It might take 100 folds to incorporate all of it. Stick with me, it's worth it!

Spoon chocolate mixture over prepared crust and smooth top. Pan will be FULL. Cover and chill at least 4 hours. You can make this cake a day ahead. Garnish with additional whipped cream, raspberries and chocolate drizzle before serving.

Makes 12 servings

Per serving (if you really must know):
450 calories, 32 g total fat (19 g saturated fat), 6 g protein, 42 g carbohydrate (2.6 g fiber, 30 g sugars), 66 mg cholesterol, 240 mg sodium

SCAN FOR VIDEO!

Wickedly *Delicious*
SPLURGE-WORTHY
Totally Worth It!

YUM
Try using half semi-sweet chocolate and half dark (60%) chocolate if you prefer a bittersweet flavor.

YUMMER!
Freezing the cake makes it taste like a decadent ice cream dessert! Add the whipped cream garnish, berries and chocolate drizzle just before serving.

Shockingly Delicious
Chocolate Avocado Pudding

GF · DF · V

Lower your raised eyebrows and give this rich-tasting, super-creamy "instant" chocolate pudding a try! A popular treat among vegans, this unusual combination of ingredients is healthy and decadent at the same time. It contains good fats and lots of fiber from avocados, antioxidants from cocoa powder and is sweetened naturally with pure maple syrup.

---

2 large ripe avocados, halved, pitted, flesh scooped out (about 2 cups avocados)
6 tbsp unsweetened cocoa powder
5 tbsp pure maple syrup*
¼ to ⅓ cup milk (dairy, almond or coconut)
Pinch fine sea salt

* I've tried this recipe using honey and found it made my pudding taste like—you guessed it—honey (instead of rich chocolate). So, I'd suggest you stick with maple syrup.

Place all ingredients into the bowl of a food processor (I use my small mini processor) and whirl until perfectly smooth. You might need to add a bit more milk if pudding is too thick.

Taste and add more maple syrup, if desired. Pudding is ready to eat immediately, but it tastes SO much better when very cold. Chilling for at least 2 hours really makes a difference. Did I mention it's better served cold?

May be stored for up to 24 hours in refrigerator. As with most recipes using avocados, you can't store this pudding too long before it starts to spoil.

Makes 4 servings

Per serving: 246 calories, 16 g total fat (2.8 g saturated fat), 4 g protein, 30 g carbohydrate (9.4 g fiber, 17 g sugars), 0 mg cholesterol, 89 mg sodium

Have you seen those giant, green, shiny-skinned fruits labeled "lite" avocados at the store? You know, the ones that appear to be half avocado and half dinosaur egg? As an avocado addict and aspiring aficionado, I'm slightly horrified by these edible imposters. "50% less fat! 35% fewer calories!" screams the sticker. So, what exactly are they? Well, turns out they aren't imposters at all. They're Florida avocados. Unfortunately, in addition to having half the fat, they also have half the flavor. I'd describe them as a watered-down version of the classic, black-skinned Hass avocado. A "diet" avocado, if you will. I won't.

SCAN FOR VIDEO!

YUM

Serve topped with sliced
strawberries or fresh raspberries.

YUMMER!

Add 2 tbsp peanut butter and
½ ripe banana. You'll need to add a
bit more milk since it'll be super thick.

Sooooo chocolaty!

Extra-Chocolaty
Chocolate Zucchini Muffins

These decadent, double-chocolate zucchini muffins with gooey, melty chocolate chips are sure to become a family favorite! Apple sauce and Greek yogurt help keep them moist, since there's very little oil in the recipe. Insanely delicious when served warm from the oven!

¾ cup plain 0% Greek yogurt

¾ cup packed light brown sugar

½ cup unsweetened applesauce

2 eggs

2 tbsp sunflower or safflower oil
  (I use organic)

1 tsp vanilla

1 cup grated unpeeled zucchini
  (pat dry with paper towels)

¾ cup all-purpose flour
  (see Kitchen Whizdom)

½ cup whole wheat flour

½ cup unsweetened cocoa powder

1½ tsp baking powder

½ tsp baking soda

½ tsp sea salt

½ cup mini semi-sweet chocolate chips

Preheat oven to 350°F. Spray a 12-cup muffin tin with cooking spray or lightly oil and set aside. (Or use paper liners.)

In a medium bowl, whisk together yogurt, sugar, applesauce, eggs, oil and vanilla until well blended. Stir in zucchini. Set aside.

In a large bowl, whisk together both flours, cocoa, baking powder, baking soda and salt until well blended. Stir in chocolate chips.

Add wet ingredients to dry ingredients and stir just until dry ingredients are moistened. Batter will be thick. Evenly spoon batter into prepared cups and bake for 20 to 22 minutes, or until a wooden pick inserted in center of muffin comes out clean (or with just a few moist crumbs). Cool on a wire rack. Serve warm.

Makes 12 muffins

Per muffin: 196 calories, 6.9 g total fat (2.4 g saturated fat), 5.7 g protein, 30 g carbohydrate (2.4 g fiber, 15 g sugars), 35 mg cholesterol, 207 mg sodium

I've successfully made these super-chocolaty muffins using three different flour options: (1) the all-purpose flour plus whole wheat flour combo specified in the recipe; (2) 1¼ cups whole wheat pastry flour, which is lighter and fluffier and less dense than regular whole wheat flour; and (3) my homemade gluten-free flour blend (recipe on page 244). When using the gluten-free flour blend, you'll likely need to increase the baking time by a few minutes. The muffins taste great but they're a bit more delicate. I've never made this recipe using commercially prepared gluten-free flour blends (they're all SO different and I've purchased many total duds!), so if you have success using one, please let me know!

SCAN FOR VIDEO!

YUM
Make these GLUTEN-FREE by using my gluten-free flour blend on page 244.

YUMMER!
Add ½ cup chopped walnuts or pecans when you add the chocolate chips.

GO LOCO FOR COCOA!

Melt-in-Your-Mouth
Flourless Peanut Butter Cookies

GF **DF**

When you want cookies fast and don't want to fuss, make this one-bowl wonder your go-to recipe. With minimum ingredients and maximum flavor, these crave-worthy cookies are a dream come true for those on a gluten-free diet.

- -

1 cup crunchy natural peanut butter

¾ cup packed brown sugar

1 tbsp flax meal (ground flaxseed) or ground chia seeds

1 large egg, lightly beaten

1 tsp baking powder

1 tsp vanilla

¼ tsp sea salt

Preheat oven to 350°F.

In a deep mixing bowl, combine all ingredients and stir thoroughly using a wooden spoon. Mixture will seem wet at first and then get very stiff. This is normal and good!

Using your hands, roll dough into 1¼-inch balls. If necessary, wet hands occasionally to prevent dough from sticking.

Place balls on an ungreased cookie sheet 2 inches apart. Press down lightly using the tines of a fork. Bake for 10 to 12 minutes. Cookies might seem underbaked but that's okay. Remove pan from oven and place on a wire rack to cool for 10 minutes. (Don't try to remove cookies from cookie sheet right out of the oven. They'll be too soft and will break.) Once partially cooled, carefully transfer cookies to wire rack to cool completely.

Makes 18 cookies

Per cookie: 126 calories, 7.7 g fat (1.2 g saturated fat), 4 g protein, 12 g carbohydrate (1 g fiber, 9 g sugars), 12 mg cholesterol, 53 mg sodium

Yes, these are high in fat, but eating one of these cookies is basically like eating a big spoonful of peanut butter, which contains good fats plus some protein. I've made these cookies with coconut sugar and they tasted great! However, they were extremely chewy so I wouldn't recommend this variation for people with dentures. Seriously!

SCAN FOR VIDEO!

YUM

I've made these cookies with sunflower butter and they were delicious!

YUMMER!

Press a few mini, semi-sweet chocolate chips into the tops of each cookie before baking.

Peanut "BETTER" cookies

NO FLOUR!

Potato Starch

MAKE YOUR OWN
Gluten-Free
FLOUR BLEND

(GF) (DF) (V)

Xanthan Gum

In a large bowl, whisk together 2 cups potato
starch (not potato flour), 2 cups sorghum flour,
½ cup coconut flour, ½ cup brown rice flour and
1 tbsp xanthan gum until well blended. Store in an
airtight container in the fridge for up to 2 months.

Makes 5 cups flour blend

Per serving (¼ cup): 140 calories,
1 g total fat (0.4 g saturated fat),
2.3 g protein, 31 g carbohydrate
(2.8 g fiber, 0 g sugars),
0 mg cholesterol, 7 mg sodium

Coconut Flour

Sorghum Flour

Brown Rice Flour

* Look for these ingredients at bulk food stores, health food stores or in the natural food section of your grocery store.

Use in "short" baked goods that don't require a lot of leavening, such as pancakes, cookies and muffins. Not recommended for bread or cakes. You may need to increase or decrease the liquid in your recipe when using gluten-free flours.

SCAN FOR VIDEO!

Grilled Peaches with Ricotta
❧ & Honey-Lemon-Ginger Syrup ❧

GF

If you've never grilled peaches before, you really should try it! Juicy, sweet peaches pair perfectly with creamy ricotta and a drizzle of flavor-infused honey. And at just over 150 calories per serving, they're a light, deliciously simple ending to a summertime meal.

Syrup

¼ cup liquid honey

¼ cup freshly squeezed lemon juice

1 tbsp minced fresh gingerroot

4 large ripe peaches
 (see Kitchen Whizdom)

1 tbsp melted butter or neutral-tasting oil

1½ cups extra-smooth ricotta cheese

¼ cup chopped fresh mint

Makes 8 servings

Per serving: 157 calories, 6.2 g total fat
(3.9 g saturated fat), 5.6 g protein,
22 g carbohydrate (1.8 g fiber, 18 g sugars),
26 mg cholesterol, 49 mg sodium

To make the syrup, whisk together honey, lemon juice and gingerroot in your smallest pot. Bring to a boil over medium-high heat. Immediately reduce heat to low and let mixture simmer, uncovered, until liquid is reduced by half and becomes syrupy. This should take no more than 5 minutes. Strain to remove gingerroot. Let syrup cool until ready to use. It'll thicken up a bit more as it cools.

Preheat grill to medium-high heat. Halve and pit peaches. Tip: Cut down the indented line of the peach and twist open like an avocado!

Brush cut sides of peaches lightly with melted butter. Grill for about 3 to 4 minutes per side, until peaches have nice grill marks and start to caramelize a bit.

Arrange peaches on a serving tray. Fluff up the ricotta and put a generous dollop on each peach half. Drizzle with syrup, sprinkle with mint and serve immediately.

Promise me you'll make this dessert only with the juiciest, tastiest, in-season peaches, otherwise you'll be disappointed with the flavor. The syrup can also double as a home remedy to help ward off sickness. Add one teaspoon syrup to hot tea when you start feeling under the weather. Honey, lemon and ginger are natural cold and flu fighters!

SCAN FOR
VIDEO!

YUM
Ripe, juicy nectarines can be substituted for peaches.

YUMMER!
A small scoop of vanilla ice cream tastes pretty darn delicious on warm, grilled peaches. Just sayin'.

DID YOU KNOW?
Nectarines are just peaches without the FUZZ!

Lemon-Blueberry Cheesecake Parfaits

GF*

When you're craving cheesecake but don't feel like turning on the oven, whip up these impressive-looking, lightened up, layered parfaits instead. Double or triple the recipe to make cute and colorful individual desserts that your party guests will love!

1½ cups lemon-flavored Greek yogurt (see Kitchen Whizdom)

3 oz (85 g) light cream cheese, at room temperature

1½ cups blueberries (fresh or frozen)

2 tbsp pure maple syrup, liquid honey or granulated sugar

1 tbsp freshly squeezed lemon juice

2 tsp cornstarch

1 cup crushed graham crackers*

Extra blueberries or raspberries or chopped strawberries for garnish (optional)

* For a gluten-free dessert, use gluten-free graham crackers or any gluten-free cookie you enjoy, crushed into crumbs.

Makes 4 servings

Per serving: 294 calories, 5.6 g total fat (2 g saturated fat), 11 g protein, 51 g carbohydrate (1.9 g fiber, 28 g sugars), 15 mg cholesterol, 295 mg sodium

In a medium bowl, beat together yogurt and cream cheese using medium speed of an electric mixer. Continue to beat until mixture is smooth and silky with no lumps. Cover and refrigerate until you're ready to assemble parfaits.

In a small pot, combine blueberries, maple syrup and 2 tbsp water. Bring mixture to a gentle boil. Cook and stir for 2 minutes or until some blueberries begin to burst. Mash blueberries with a potato masher but leave mixture a little lumpy.

In a small bowl, whisk together lemon juice and cornstarch until smooth. Add to blueberry mixture and give it a good stir. Cook for 1 more minute, until mixture is bubbly and has thickened. Remove blueberry sauce from heat and let cool completely before using. It will thicken even more as it cools.

To assemble parfaits, spoon 3 tbsp graham crumbs into each of 4 small glasses. Top each with ¼ cup yogurt mixture, followed by ¼ cup blueberry sauce and another ¼ cup yogurt mixture (see photo). If there's any sauce left, spoon it over top, then sprinkle with 1 tbsp graham crumbs. Garnish with extra berries, if using. Cover and chill at least 2 hours before serving.

Can't find lemon-flavored Greek yogurt? No worries. Just combine 1½ cups plain 2% Greek yogurt with 2 tbsp honey, 1 tbsp freshly squeezed lemon juice and ½ tsp grated lemon zest. Using Greek yogurt (versus regular yogurt) means this dessert contains protein, not just carbs, which is a bonus! Make sure you allow a couple hours for chilling for the best result. Even better, prepare these pretty parfaits a day in advance, cover and refrigerate until ready to serve.

SCAN FOR VIDEO!

YUM
Try making the sauce with chopped, fresh strawberries when they're in season.

YUMMER!
For a splurge-worthy treat, use crushed shortbread cookies instead of graham crackers.

Berry DELICIOUS!

Whole Wheat Pumpkin Biscuits
with Maple-Cinnamon Butter

These fluffy, buttery biscuits with subtle pumpkin flavor are perfect for fall brunch or Thanksgiving dinner. But after just one maple-cinnamony bite, I think you'll be pumped for pumpkin all year round!

Maple-Cinnamon Butter

⅓ cup butter, softened

1 tbsp pure maple syrup

½ tsp ground cinnamon

Biscuits

¾ cup canned pure pumpkin
  (not pumpkin pie filling)

½ cup buttermilk or plain yogurt

2 tbsp pure maple syrup

1¾ cups whole wheat pastry flour*

2 tsp baking powder

1 tsp baking soda

½ tsp sea salt

½ tsp ground cinnamon

¼ cup frozen butter

* If you don't have whole wheat pastry flour, use 1 cup all-purpose flour + ¾ cup whole wheat flour.

Makes 10 biscuits

Per biscuit: 141 calories, 5 g total fat (3 g saturated fat), 2.8 g protein, 21 g carbohydrate (3.4 g fiber, 3.9 g sugars), 13 mg cholesterol, 290 mg sodium

Per 1-tsp butter: 32 calories, 3.2 g total fat (2 g saturated fat), 0 g protein, 0.8 g carbohydrate (0 g fiber, 0.8 g sugars), 9 mg cholesterol, 26 mg sodium

In a small bowl, combine butter, maple syrup and cinnamon. Mix well and set aside.

Preheat oven to 400°F. Line a baking sheet with parchment paper and set aside.

In a medium bowl, whisk together pumpkin, buttermilk and maple syrup. Set aside.

In a large bowl, combine flour, baking powder, baking soda, salt and cinnamon. Mix well. Using the large holes of a box grater, shred the butter directly into flour mixture. Stir gently (fluff it!) until the butter is evenly distributed in the flour mixture. Avoid using your hands for this purpose since they'll warm (melt!) the butter which *no es bueno*. (Practicing my Spanish.)

Pour wet ingredients into flour mixture and stir just until dry ingredients are moistened. Dough will be sticky—this is normal for biscuits! Add a bit more flour if needed until mixture forms a ball. Transfer dough to a lightly floured surface.

Pat dough into ¾-inch thickness and cut into 2½-inch rounds using a biscuit or cookie cutter. Re-roll scraps of dough to make 10 biscuits total. Transfer biscuits to prepared pan. Bake for 12 to 15 minutes, or until biscuits have puffed up and are light golden brown. Be careful not to overbake the biscuits. Serve warm with maple-cinnamon butter.

SCAN FOR VIDEO!

YUM
Use well-mashed, cooked sweet potatoes instead of pumpkin. (You might need to add a bit more liquid.)

YUMMER!
Add ½ cup shredded old (sharp) cheddar cheese to the dry ingredients. Omit cinnamon and maple-cinnamon butter. Serve with soup and stew!

Everything-but-the-Kitchen-Sink
Pumpkin Banana Zucchini Loaf

Pumpkin and banana might sound like an odd flavor pairing, but they're a match made in baking heaven! This lip-smacking loaf is super moist and delicious, yet not overly sweet. Serve with a cup of tea for an afternoon snack.

1 cup each whole wheat flour and all-purpose flour

¼ cup flax meal (ground flaxseed)

2 tsp baking powder

1 tsp baking soda

1 tsp ground cinnamon

½ tsp sea salt

1 cup mashed super-ripe bananas

1 cup canned pure pumpkin (not pumpkin pie filling)

1 cup grated unpeeled zucchini (pat dry with paper towels)

½ cup plain 2% Greek yogurt or coconut yogurt (for dairy-free)

½ cup light brown sugar (not packed)

¼ cup sunflower or safflower oil (I use organic)

1 egg

1 cup chopped pecans or walnuts

Preheat oven to 350°F. Spray a 9 x 5-inch loaf pan with cooking spray or lightly oil. Set aside.

In a medium bowl, whisk together both flours, flax meal, baking powder, baking soda, cinnamon and salt. Set aside.

In a large bowl, whisk together bananas, pumpkin, zucchini, yogurt, sugar, oil and egg until well blended. Add dry ingredients and mix using a wooden spoon just until dry ingredients are moistened. Don't overmix. Fold in nuts.

Spoon batter evenly into prepared pan. Bake for 60 minutes, or until a wooden pick inserted in center of loaf comes out clean. Remove loaf from pan and cool on a wire rack. Tastes great served warm or cold. Wrap leftovers well with plastic wrap and store in the refrigerator for up to 5 days. May be frozen.

Makes 1 large loaf, 12 slices

Per slice: 254 calories, 12 g total fat (1 g saturated fat), 7 g protein, 31 g carbohydrate (4.3 g fiber, 9 g sugars), 19 mg cholesterol, 230 mg sodium

Make sure your bananas are overripe, with lots of brown spots, for this recipe, otherwise your loaf will be lacking delicious banana flavor and sweetness. Also, please don't use an 8 x 4-inch loaf pan…it's too small and the batter won't cook properly. To accurately determine the size of your pan, always measure inside edge to inside edge, so you don't include the thickness of the pan in your measurement.

SCAN FOR VIDEO!

YUM

You can replace the grated zucchini with grated carrots for a flavor variation.

YUMMER!

For a sweeter loaf, use ½ cup walnuts or pecans + ½ cup dark chocolate chips.

FALL IN Loaf with PUMPKIN!

Greek Yogurt Lemon-Raspberry Scones
with Lemon Glaze

I love the sunny specks of yellow lemon zest in these spring-like, super-light raspberry scones. Traditionally made with loads of butter and cream, I've lightened them up with Greek yogurt and cut back on the butter without cutting back on flavor. Using frozen butter makes them lighter and fluffier!

Scones

1 cup vanilla-flavored Greek yogurt

1 egg

3 tbsp freshly squeezed lemon juice

2 tsp grated lemon zest

1½ cups all-purpose flour

¾ cup whole wheat flour

¼ cup granulated sugar or light brown sugar (not packed)

2 tsp baking powder

1 tsp baking soda

½ tsp sea salt

¼ cup frozen butter

1 cup frozen raspberries*

Glaze

½ cup icing (confectioner's) sugar

1 tbsp freshly squeezed lemon juice

1 tbsp butter, melted

½ tsp grated lemon zest

* Frozen raspberries are best because they don't break as easily as fresh berries.

Makes 12 scones

Per scone (with glaze): 200 calories, 5.5 g total fat (3 g saturated fat), 5.4 g protein, 32 g carbohydrate (2.6 fiber, 12 g sugars), 30 mg cholesterol, 218 mg sodium

Preheat oven to 400°F. Lightly oil a large cookie sheet or line with parchment paper and set aside.

In a medium bowl, whisk together yogurt, egg, lemon juice and zest. Set aside.

In a large bowl, mix together both flours until well blended. Remove ¼ cup flour blend to use for dusting work surface later. You will be left with 2 cups flour blend in bowl; to this add sugar, baking powder, baking soda and salt. Mix well. Using the large holes of a box grater, shred the butter directly into flour mixture. Stir gently (fluff it!) until the butter is evenly distributed in the flour mixture. Avoid using your hands for this purpose since they'll warm (melt!) the butter.

Pour wet ingredients into dry ingredients and mix using a wooden spoon until a soft dough forms. If dough is too stiff, add a bit more yogurt. If too sticky, add a bit more flour. Fold in raspberries. It's okay if the raspberries break a little.

Turn dough out onto a lightly floured surface. Divide dough in half and form each half into a ball. Place both dough balls on prepared cookie sheet. Pat each ball into a 1-inch-thick circle, about 6 to 7 inches in diameter, spaced at least 2 inches apart. Using a large, sharp knife, cut each circle into 6 wedges, but don't separate them. Brush tops lightly with a bit more melted butter, if desired.

Bake scones for about 18 minutes, until puffed up and golden. Transfer scones to a wire rack to cool slightly while you make the glaze. Combine glaze ingredients in a small bowl and mix well until very smooth. Pull scones apart and drizzle glaze over them. The glaze will firm up if the scones are left to sit for a few minutes, or you can eat them right away.

SCAN FOR VIDEO!

The glaze will amaze!

YUM
Try these scones with fresh blueberries instead of raspberries.

YUMMER!
For decadent, splurge-worthy scones, use heavy (whipping) cream instead of yogurt and add ½ tsp vanilla to wet ingredients.

CHAPTER 10

Good

MORNINGS

Breakfasts, smoothies and other random, tasty stuff!

YUM & YUMMER

Maple-Cinnamon Almond Butter
with Roasted Almonds

There's nuttin' better than homemade almond butter, especially when it's naturally sweetened with maple syrup and deliciously flavored with a hint of cinnamon and vanilla.

2 cups raw, natural almonds

3 tbsp pure maple syrup

1 tbsp good-quality oil
(such as organic sunflower
or melted coconut oil)

½ tsp ground cinnamon

½ tsp vanilla

¼ tsp sea salt (or to taste)

Makes about 1 cup almond butter

Per serving (1 tbsp): 97 calories,
7.9 g total fat (0.6 g saturated fat), 3 g protein,
4.9 g carbohydrate (1.7 g fiber, 2.7 g sugars),
0 mg cholesterol, 53 mg sodium

Preheat oven to 325°F. Line a small baking sheet (10 x 15 inches is perfect) with parchment paper.

In a medium bowl, mix together almonds and maple syrup until every almond is coated with syrup. Spread almonds on prepared pan in a single layer. Use a rubber spatula to scrape all of the maple syrup out of the bowl and drizzle it on top. Roast almonds for 20 minutes, stirring once about halfway through cooking time. Remove from oven and let cool on pan for 10 minutes. Processing the almonds when they're warm (not hot!) is important.

Process almonds in a food processor (fitted with "S" blade or all-purpose blade), starting with the pulse feature, until your almonds resemble bread crumbs. Add oil. Switch to high power and process almonds until they're smooth and creamy, stopping to scrape down the bowl every minute or so. Be patient. This could take 5 minutes or 15 minutes, depending on your food processor. If, after 15 minutes, you aren't looking at smooth and creamy almond butter, add more oil by the teaspoonful until desired consistency is reached. Once creamy, add cinnamon, vanilla and sea salt. Process again until well blended. Store almond butter in a sealed container in the fridge for up to 3 weeks.

You'll need a high-quality food processor or powerful blender (such as a Vitamix or Blendtec) to make this almond butter. Mini food processors (sometimes called "mini choppers") don't work well for making nut butters. Though I LOVE my blender, I prefer making nut butters using a food processor. Anyone who has the patience to scrape out the nut butter hiding underneath those pointy blender blades deserves a culinary medal of honor! If using a blender, follow the manufacturer's directions for processing nuts into nut butters.

SCAN FOR VIDEO!

YUM
Serve with apple slices for dunking or slather on a banana for breakfast.

YUMMER!
Use this nut butter to make Almond Butter Energy Bites, page 230.

Go NUTS for almond butter!

Best-Ever
Homemade Almond Milk

GF **DF** **V**

With a hint of vanilla and touch of cinnamon, you'll never go back to store-bought almond milk once you try this simple, deliciously creamy, homemade version.

---

1 cup raw, natural almonds

6 cups cold filtered water, divided

3 pitted dates or 2 tbsp pure maple syrup

1 tsp vanilla

½ tsp ground cinnamon

Pinch sea salt

Nut milk bag or other thin cloth for straining
   (see Kitchen Whizdom)

Makes 4 to 5 cups almond milk

Per serving (½ cup): 53 calories, 3.6 g total fat
(0.3 g saturated fat), 1.5 g protein, 4 g carbohydrate
(0.9 g fiber, 3 g sugars), 0 mg cholesterol, 28 mg sodium

Place almonds in a glass bowl and cover completely with 2 cups water. Add a pinch of sea salt to the water. Refrigerate and let soak overnight or at least 12 hours. Drain almonds and rinse well.

Place soaked almonds, 3 cups water, dates, vanilla, cinnamon and sea salt in a high-powered blender. Blend on lowest speed for about 10 seconds, then gradually increase speed to high and blend for one full minute.

Use a nut milk bag (or a fine mesh sieve lined with a couple layers of cheesecloth) to strain the milk. Squeeze or press down on the almond pulp to extract as much milk as possible. (Watch the video!) Discard the solids.

Thin the nut milk with water to reach your desired consistency. I usually add at least 1 cup water at this point. Transfer milk to an airtight container and chill until cold. Lasts about 3 days in the fridge.

KITCHEN WHIZDOM

Soaking the nuts results in a creamier, smoother texture. Don't skip this step! I use Medjool dates, which are large, plump and caramelly. You'll find nut milk bags at health-food stores or online. Sadly, my nut milk bag broke the first time I used it, likely from my aggressive squeezing to extract every last drop of milk. So, I switched to a thin, white cloth napkin (Clean! No fabric softener or dryer-sheet residue, please!), which worked great. Finally, if you think it's wasteful to throw away the leftover almond pulp, just Google "uses for almond pulp" and you'll find dozens of ideas!

SCAN FOR VIDEO!

make your own
ALMOND MILK

YUM
Add a TINY pinch of nutmeg along with the cinnamon.

YUMMER!
Serve with Pumpkin Spice Granola, page 280, and enjoy your time in breakfast heaven!

Avocado & Smoked Salmon Toasts
with Cucumber Ribbons

Avocado toast is easy like Sunday morning, which is usually when I make it. And just because something's super simple, doesn't mean it has to be bland or boring. These toasts are filling and satisfying, containing good fats from the avocado and lots of protein via the smoked salmon.

1 medium ripe avocado

1 tbsp freshly squeezed lemon juice

Sea salt and freshly ground black pepper

2 slices grainy bread or 1 grainy, seedy
   bagel, halved

1 small cucumber, cut into paper-thin ribbons
   (see Kitchen Whizdom)

2 paper-thin red onion slices (see Kitchen Whizdom)

2 oz (57 g) wild smoked salmon

Sprouts or microgreens or fresh dill sprigs
   for garnish (optional)

Halve avocado, remove pit and scoop out flesh into a small bowl. Add lemon juice and a couple grinds of salt and pepper. Mash well with a fork, leaving a few lumps. Set aside.

Toast bread until nice 'n' toasty (so it won't go soggy after topping with avocado!). Spread half the avocado mixture over each piece of toast. Top with cucumber ribbons and onion slices, followed by salmon and sprouts, if using. Serve immediately.

Makes 2 servings

Per serving: 265 calories, 12.4 g total fat (1.9 g saturated fat), 14.3 g protein, 24 g carbohydrate (9.4 g fiber, 2.2 g sugars), 20 mg cholesterol, 586 mg sodium

To take the sharpness or "bite" out of raw onions and prevent them from overpowering a recipe (or a salad or burger), try this trick: Soak the onion slices in ice-cold water for at least 10 minutes, then drain and dry them on paper towels before using. Ice-cold water keeps the onions crunchy but mellows their flavor. To make cucumber ribbons, simply run your vegetable peeler down the length of an unpeeled cucumber. (I like the green edge! See photo.) You'll toss out the first couple slices since they'll be mostly peel. Still not sure? Watch the video!

SCAN FOR VIDEO!

Microgreens/
sprouts

Cucumber
ribbons

Red onions

Smoked salmon

Mashed
avocado

❧ 5-Minute ❧
Cinnamon Bun Oatmeal

GF

This tasty breakfast treat will warm you up on a cold winter's morning! And it's so simple and quick to make. The chia seeds and pecans add good fats, while the mashed banana lends natural sweetness. A cinnamon-bun-lover's dream!

Oatmeal

1 cup milk of choice (dairy, almond, etc.)
½ cup quick-cooking oats (not instant)*
½ small RIPE banana, mashed
  (see Kitchen Whizdom)
1 tbsp chia, flax or hemp seeds
½ tsp ground cinnamon
Pinch sea salt

Topping

2 tsp pure maple syrup
½ tsp ground cinnamon
2 tbsp vanilla-flavored Greek yogurt
3 pecans, chopped

* For gluten-free, make sure you use certified gluten-free oats.

In a small saucepan, heat milk over medium-high heat until barely simmering. Reduce heat to low. Add oats, banana, chia, cinnamon and salt. Cook and stir for 3 minutes or until oats reach desired consistency. Remove from heat and spoon into a serving bowl.

In a small bowl, combine maple syrup and cinnamon. Mix well. Drizzle maple-cinnamon mixture and yogurt over oatmeal. Top with chopped pecans. Serve hot.

Makes 1 serving

Per serving (made with unsweetened almond milk):
396 calories, 13 g total fat (1.2 g saturated fat), 12 g protein, 62 g carbohydrate (13 g fiber, 19 g sugars), 0 mg cholesterol, 471 mg sodium

Since childhood, I've always considered oatmeal to be an ultra-boring, snooze-a-rama, lame excuse of a breakfast. And that's me being polite! Then I started experimenting with creative topping options (toptions) and voilà! Breakfast was suddenly oat of this world! My favorite toptions: (1) Diced banana with a drizzle of natural almond butter or peanut butter and a sprinkle of shredded coconut or sliced almonds; (2) Fresh blueberries or raspberries with a generous dollop of vanilla-flavored Greek yogurt; and (3) Diced apples that I've sautéed in a bit of butter until softened, topped with a sprinkle of coconut sugar or brown sugar and cinnamon. Do you have a favorite way to top oatmeal? I'd love to hear about it!

SCAN FOR VIDEO!

YUM
Try coconut sugar or brown sugar instead of maple syrup.

YUMMER!
Omit the pecans and drizzle warmed almond butter or peanut butter over the oatmeal. Delish!

OATstanding flavor!

BYOB: Build Your Own Bowl

GF DF V

For anyone not familiar with a smoothie bowl, let me explain. It's a smoothie. In a bowl. Okay, now that we've cleared that up, let's do this! Often! Smoothie bowls are DELISH and so pretty. I make mine extra thick (start with frozen fruit!) so I can pile on the healthy toppings.

Base

Option 1: Tropical Vegan

1 cup frozen mango chunks

1 cup frozen banana chunks

1 cup unsweetened dairy-free coconut yogurt

2 tbsp pure maple syrup

Almond milk or other nut milk to make it blendable

Small scoop vanilla protein powder (optional)

Option 2: Strawberry Banana (pictured)

1 cup frozen strawberries

1 cup frozen banana chunks

1 cup plain 0% Greek yogurt

2 tbsp liquid honey or pure maple syrup

Milk (any kind) to make it blendable

Toppings

Fresh berries	**Flaxseeds**
Sliced bananas	**Pumpkin seeds**
Any fruit, really	**Sunflower seeds**
Shredded coconut	**Granola**
Hemp seeds	**Chopped nuts**
Chia seeds	**Leftover ham (joking!)**

Combine all base ingredients in a high-powered blender and whirl until smooth. You may need to stop the blender and scrape down the sides once or twice since mixture is very thick.

Divide smoothie mixture among serving bowls and garnish with desired toppings. Serve immediately while super cold!

Makes 2 servings

Per serving (Tropical Vegan, base only): 219 calories, 4.7 g total fat (3.4 g saturated fat), 2 g protein, 46 g carbohydrate (4 g fiber, 33 g sugars), 0 mg cholesterol, 47 mg sodium

Per serving (Strawberry Banana, base only): 229 calories, 0.7 g total fat (0.3 g saturated fat), 14 g protein, 46 g carbohydrate (3.1 g fiber, 29 g sugars), 12 mg cholesterol, 60 mg sodium

SCAN FOR VIDEO!

A smoothie in a bowl

Carrot Cake Pancakes
～ with Creamy Maple-Orange Topping ～

For a special occasion or holiday brunch, wow your guests with these mouthwatering pancakes served with a dreamy, creamy topping (made with Greek yogurt!).

Topping

1½ cups plain 0% Greek yogurt

3 tbsp pure maple syrup

½ tsp grated orange zest

Pancakes

1 cup all-purpose flour

½ cup whole wheat flour

2 tsp ground cinnamon

1 tsp baking powder

½ tsp each baking soda and sea salt

¼ tsp each ground nutmeg and ground ginger

1⅔ cups buttermilk

1 cup cooked, mashed carrots
  (see Kitchen Whizdom)

3 tbsp pure maple syrup + extra for serving (optional)

2 tbsp sunflower or safflower oil (or melted butter)

1 egg

1 tsp vanilla

½ cup each chopped walnuts and unsweetened
  shredded coconut

In a small bowl, combine all topping ingredients and mix well. Refrigerate until serving time.

Preheat electric griddle to medium-high heat. To make pancakes, combine both flours, cinnamon, baking powder, baking soda, salt, nutmeg and ginger in a large bowl. Mix well.

In a medium bowl, whisk together buttermilk, carrots, maple syrup, oil, egg and vanilla. Add wet ingredients to dry ingredients and mix just until dry ingredients are moistened. Stir in walnuts and coconut.

Lightly oil griddle or spray with cooking spray. For each pancake, spoon about ⅓ cup batter onto griddle and spread to make a 4-inch circle. Cook until undersides are lightly browned, about 2 minutes. Flip pancakes over and continue to cook for 2 to 3 more minutes. Top warm pancakes with yogurt topping (and extra maple syrup, if desired).

Makes 12 pancakes

Per pancake (with 2 tbsp topping): 203 calories, 7.8 g total fat (3.5 g saturated fat), 8 g protein, 26 g carbohydrate (2.2 g fiber, 10 g sugars), 25 mg cholesterol, 176 mg sodium

Many carrot cake pancake recipes call for raw, finely grated carrots, which won't cook properly in the short time it takes to make pancakes. The solution is to cook the carrots first. Just steam or boil them until tender, allow them to cool, then mash them really well with a fork.

SCAN FOR VIDEO!

YUM

Try chopped pecans instead of walnuts. Toasting them adds a bit more flavor.

YUMMER!

Take the topping over the top! Use 1 cup yogurt + ½ cup light cream cheese. Beat well with an electric mixer until smooth, then add the maple syrup and orange zest.

JOY TO THE
Whirled!
Start your day the smoothie way

Pumpkin Pie Protein Smoothie

(GF) (DF) (V)

A delicious, on-the-go breakfast or snack with warm spices, good fats and protein!

1½ cups ice-cold water
½ cup canned pure pumpkin
   (not pumpkin pie filling)
1 scoop vanilla protein powder*
1 small frozen ripe banana, cut into chunks
1 tbsp almond butter or peanut butter
1 tbsp ground chia seeds (use whole seeds
   if you have a powerful blender)
1 tsp pumpkin pie spice
A few ice cubes

Makes 1 serving

Per serving: 346 calories, 12.4 g total fat (1 g saturated fat), 23 g protein, 42 g carbohydrate (11 g fiber, 18 g sugars), 0 mg cholesterol, 148 mg sodium

Directions:
Place all ingredients in a high-powered blender and whirl until smooth. Serve immediately.

* If you don't like protein powder, use ¾ cup vanilla-flavored Greek yogurt (non-vegan). Add a bit more water if the smoothie is too thick.

YUM

SCAN FOR VIDEO!

Blueberry Muffin Breakfast Smoothie

Ditch your morning muffin and drink
this healthy smoothie version instead!

1 cup unsweetened almond milk (or dairy milk)
½ cup frozen blueberries
1 small frozen ripe banana, cut into chunks
¼ cup quick-cooking oats
1 scoop vanilla protein powder*
1 tbsp chia seeds or hemp seeds (for omega-3s!)
Dash cinnamon

Makes 1 serving

Per serving: 341 calories, 7.8 g total fat (0.6 g saturated fat),
22 g protein, 50 g carbohydrate (10.6 fiber, 18 g sugars),
0 mg cholesterol, 322 mg sodium

SCAN FOR VIDEO!

Directions:
Place all ingredients in a
high-powered blender and whirl
until smooth. Serve immediately.

* If you don't like protein powder,
use ¾ cup vanilla-flavored
Greek yogurt (non-vegan).
Add a bit more milk if the
smoothie is too thick.

Chocolate, Peanut Butter & Banana Smoothie

Tastes so good, you'd think it was dessert, not breakfast!

1 cup unsweetened almond milk
  (or dairy milk or water)
1 tbsp natural peanut butter
1 tbsp chia seeds or hemp seeds
1 small frozen ripe banana,
  cut into chunks
1 scoop chocolate protein powder*
A few ice cubes

Makes 1 serving

Per serving: 356 calories, 13.8 g total fat
(1.6 g saturated fat), 22 g protein, 39 g carbohydrate
(8 g fiber, 20.8 g sugars), 0 mg cholesterol, 331 mg sodium

Directions:

Place all ingredients in a high-powered
blender and whirl until smooth.
Serve immediately.

* If you don't like protein powder, use
¾ cup vanilla-flavored Greek yogurt
(non-vegan). Add a bit more milk if
the smoothie is too thick.

SCAN FOR
VIDEO!

Tropikale Sunshine Smoothie

A.K.A. my "Greena Colada" smoothie, it's creamy, delicious and reminds me of a beach vacation.

1 can (14 oz/398 mL) light coconut milk
½ cup frozen pineapple chunks
½ cup frozen mango chunks
1 small frozen ripe banana, cut into chunks
1 tbsp chia seeds or hemp seeds
Small handful baby kale leaves

Makes 2 servings

SCAN FOR VIDEO!

Directions:

Place all ingredients in a high-powered blender and whirl until smooth. Serve immediately.

Per serving: 275 calories, 15.8 g total fat (10.7 g saturated fat), 3 g protein, 30 g carbohydrate (4 g fiber, 18 g sugars), 0 mg cholesterol, 58 mg sodium

Apple-Cinnamon Breakfast Quinoa

It's time to think outside the cereal box when it comes to breakfast! Quinoa fans will love this warm, creamy, hearty breakfast that's slightly sweet and totally satisfying!

---

2 tsp butter or vegan buttery spread

1 cup diced unpeeled apples (red-skinned apples look nice!)

¾ cup unsweetened almond milk (or dairy milk)

2 tbsp dried currants or raisins

2 tbsp sliced almonds

2 tsp coconut sugar, pure maple syrup or liquid honey

½ tsp each ground cinnamon and vanilla

1½ cups cooked quinoa

Melt butter in a small (7-inch), non-stick skillet over medium heat. Add apples. Cook and stir for about 2 minutes, until apples begin to soften.

Add milk, currants, almonds, coconut sugar, cinnamon and vanilla. Mix well and cook until bubbly around edges but not boiling. Add cooked quinoa. Continue to cook, stirring often, until some of the milk has been absorbed and mixture thickens, about 2 minutes.

Serve hot topped with more cinnamon, if desired.

Makes 2 servings

Per serving: 344 calories, 10.8 g total fat (3 g saturated fat), 8 g protein, 54 g carbohydrate (7.5 g fiber, 20 g sugars), 10 mg cholesterol, 81 mg sodium

I'm keen about quinoa and here's why: It's one of the few complete sources of plant protein, containing all 9 essential amino acids. The fact that it's gluten-free is a bonus. I love that it cooks in about 15 minutes and has a slightly nutty flavor. It's nutritious, too, since it's a good source of magnesium, potassium, zinc, iron and antioxidants. Tip: You should rinse quinoa before cooking it to remove the outer coating, called saponin, which has a bitter, unpleasant taste. Or, look for quinoa that's sold pre-rinsed, which is quinoawesome! (And just in case you're a newbie to the quinoa scene, it's pronounced "keen-wah" not "qwin-oh-ah.")

SCAN FOR VIDEO!

YUM
Try dried blueberries instead of currants.

YUMMER!
Top with a generous dollop of vanilla-flavored Greek yogurt.

Plant-based & protein-packed

Fluffy & Fabulous
Coconut & Banana Pancakes

In my humble opinion, these might be the best gluten-free and dairy-free pancakes you'll ever taste. Big and fluffy, full of flavor and super easy to make…this recipe's forkin' fantastic!

2 cups gluten-free flour blend (see recipe, page 244)*

2 tsp baking powder

½ tsp each ground cinnamon and sea salt

1 can (14 oz/398 mL) coconut milk (light or regular; see Kitchen Whizdom)

1½ cups mashed super-ripe bananas

2 eggs

2 tbsp pure maple syrup + extra for serving (optional)

½ tsp vanilla

* You can use 1⅓ cups all-purpose flour plus ⅔ cup whole wheat flour instead of the gluten-free flour blend.

Makes 10 large pancakes

Per pancake: 227 calories, 7.2 g total fat (5.6 g saturated fat), 4 g protein, 36 g carbohydrate (3.1 g fiber, 7.8 g sugars), 37 mg cholesterol, 195 mg sodium

Preheat electric griddle to medium-high heat.

In a large bowl, combine flour blend, baking powder, cinnamon and salt. Mix well.

In a medium bowl, whisk together coconut milk, bananas (super-ripe, right?), eggs, maple syrup and vanilla until well blended. Add wet ingredients to dry ingredients and mix just until dry ingredients are moistened.

Lightly oil griddle or spray with cooking spray. For each pancake, spoon about ⅓ cup batter onto griddle and spread to make a 4-inch circle. Cook until undersides are lightly browned, about 2 minutes. Flip pancakes over and continue to cook for 2 to 3 more minutes. Top warm pancakes with additional maple syrup, if desired.

Since this recipe doesn't contain added oil or butter like most pancake recipes, I use full-fat coconut milk instead of light for maximum flavor (but the choice is yours!). Did you know leftover pancakes freeze well? Place small sheets of parchment between them for easy separation, them wrap 'em up tightly in plastic wrap. I've kept pancakes frozen for two months without any issue. Reheat them in the microwave or in a 375°F oven or toaster oven. For oven method, cover the pancakes with foil to prevent them from drying out.

SCAN FOR VIDEO!

WOW

YUM
If dairy isn't a problem and you don't care for coconut milk, use buttermilk. Add ½ tsp baking soda to the dry ingredients.

YUMMER!
Top with sliced bananas and toasted coconut (pictured) for a splurge-worthy treat.

Not a single serving :)

Nicaragua Bowl
~ with Brown Rice, Beans, Eggs & Avocado ~

One of my best vacations ever was taking part in a surf and yoga retreat* held in breathtaking Nicaragua. The sun, the beach, the vibe, the warm ocean, the people, the FOOD! I'd go back in a heartbeat, especially for the daily breakfast feature that all of us devoured, known as the Nicaragua Bowl (or Nica Bowl, for short).

3 tsp butter, divided

½ cup diced onions

1½ cups cooked brown rice

½ cup cooked black beans (canned or frozen)

¾ tsp each ground cumin and chili powder

1 tbsp freshly squeezed lime juice

1 tbsp minced fresh cilantro

2 eggs

½ medium avocado, sliced

½ cup salsa (I like it hot!)

¼ cup shredded part-skim old (sharp) cheddar
    cheese (1 oz/28 g)

Makes 2 servings

Per serving: 486 calories, 21 g total fat (8 g saturated fat),
19 g protein, 55 g carbohydrate (10.4 g fiber, 5 g sugars),
211 mg cholesterol, 496 mg sodium

* My incredible, unforgettable retreat was organized and led by Sandra Tedeschi of Vajra Sol Yoga Adventures. Look her up and you'll probably find me in her website photo gallery, falling off a surfboard, holding a yoga pose or drinking a piña colada. ☺

In a small, non-stick skillet, heat 1 tsp butter over medium heat. Add onions. Cook and stir until onions are tender, about 3 minutes.

Add rice, beans, cumin and chili powder to onions in skillet. Mix well, until rice and beans are coated with seasonings. Stir in lime juice and 2 tbsp water. Cook and stir for 1 more minute. Remove from heat and stir in cilantro. Divide mixture in half and transfer to two serving bowls, cover and keep warm.

Wipe skillet clean and cook the eggs. Heat remaining 2 tsp butter in skillet over medium heat until it's foamy. Crack the eggs and gently add them to the skillet. Cook until the whites are set and start to brown a bit around the edges. Slide a spatula under eggs and gently flip. Cook for 30 more seconds.

Remove eggs from skillet and place over rice and bean mixture in each bowl. Arrange sliced avocados beside the eggs, then add a dollop of salsa and a sprinkle of cheese. Serve immediately.

SCAN FOR VIDEO!

YUM
Any egg will do!
Scrambled, over easy,
sunny-side up
or hard-boiled.

YUMMER!
Tastes particularly
scrumptious when made
with guacamole instead
of sliced avocados.

TASTES UNBELIEVA-BOWL!

Pumpkin Spice Granola

GF · DF · V

You many never buy pre-made granola again after you try this fabulous recipe! Crunchy, delicious and flavored with fall spices, a little bowla granola makes a healthy snack or quick breakfast.

3 cups old-fashioned oats
   (see Kitchen Whizdom)
1 cup chopped nuts (almonds, pecans,
   walnuts, pistachios or a combination)
1 cup unsweetened large-flake coconut
½ cup pumpkin seeds
¼ cup flaxseeds
½ cup pure maple syrup
½ cup canned pure pumpkin
   (not pumpkin pie filling)
¼ cup coconut oil or butter
3 tbsp coconut sugar or brown sugar
1 tbsp pumpkin pie spice
1 tsp ground cinnamon
1 tsp vanilla
¼ tsp sea salt
¾ cup dried cranberries

Makes about 7 cups granola

Per serving (⅓ cup): 194 calories, 10 g total fat
(4 g saturated fat), 4 g protein, 22 g carbohydrate
(3.3 g fiber, 10 g sugars), 6 mg cholesterol, 16 mg sodium

Preheat oven to 325°F. Line a large sheet pan with parchment paper and set aside. (Or use two smaller pans.)

In a large bowl, combine oats, nuts, coconut, pumpkin seeds and flaxseeds (do not add cranberries). Mix well.

In a medium pot, combine maple syrup, pumpkin, coconut oil, sugar, spices, vanilla and salt. Cook and stir over medium heat until coconut oil is melted and sugar is dissolved. Pour maple-pumpkin mixture over oat mixture. Mix well, until no dry oats remain. This may take a minute or two of stirring.

Transfer wet granola mixture to prepared pan and spread as thinly and evenly as possible. Bake for 30 to 35 minutes, carefully removing pan from oven and stirring granola every 10 minutes. This will ensure even baking. Cook until granola looks "toasty" and golden, but not brown.

Remove pan from oven and let granola cool completely. Add cranberries and store in an airtight container for 1 week. (I keep my granola in the fridge to prolong its freshness.)

Old-fashioned oats are sometimes called large-flake oats. They're bigger and thicker than quick-cooking oats and are better suited to making granola. For gluten-free, make sure your bag of oats says "certified gluten-free" on it or contact the manufacturer to be certain. If you despise coconut (I love it!), replace the flaked coconut with more nuts and seeds (sunflower seeds would work well). It's important to keep the dry volume the same or your granola may be too wet or too dry. Baking time will vary depending on your pan sizes, so keep checking and stirring often. The granola should feel dry to the touch and look golden brown when removed from the oven. Be careful not to burn it!

SCAN FOR VIDEO!

YUM
Use butter instead of coconut oil and raisins instead of cranberries.

YUMMER!
Try it with my homemade almond milk, page 260. So good!

Yumola!

Grilled Vegetable Frittata
✤ with Basil & Feta ✤

**Sunday brunch is the perfect occasion for this gorgeous, veggie-filled frittata.
It's colorful, flavorful and one-dish wonderful!**

4 cups chopped grilled vegetables
(see Kitchen Whizdom)

½ cup crumbled light or regular feta cheese
(2 oz/57 g)

¼ cup chopped fresh basil or
2 tbsp minced fresh dill

10 large eggs

½ cup 2% milk or half-and-half (10%) cream

¼ cup freshly grated Parmesan cheese

½ tsp each sea salt and freshly ground
black pepper

Tiny tomatoes on the vine to make it look pretty
(see photo; optional)

Makes 6 servings

Per serving: 224 calories, 13.7 g total fat (4.7 g saturated fat),
17 g protein, 10 g carbohydrate (2.6 g fiber, 5 g sugars),
318 mg cholesterol, 501 mg sodium

You'll need a 9-inch, deep-dish casserole (round or square) or a deep, 9- or 10-inch, ovenproof skillet for this recipe.

Preheat oven to 375°F. Lightly oil casserole dish or skillet (or spray with cooking spray). Spread grilled vegetables evenly over bottom of dish. Sprinkle with feta and basil.

In a medium bowl or large measuring cup, whisk together eggs, milk, Parmesan, salt and pepper until well blended. Pour egg mixture over vegetables. Bake, uncovered, on middle oven rack for about 30 minutes, or until puffed up and set in the middle. Turn on the broiler and broil frittata for about 1 minute, until light golden brown on top. Be careful not to burn it! NOTE: If using tiny tomatoes, place them on top of the frittata before broiling.

Carefully remove frittata from oven and let stand for 5 minutes before serving. Serve with fresh fruit, sliced tomatoes or a green salad.

KITCHEN WHIZDOM

If using a skillet for this recipe, make sure it can safely go in the oven and under the broiler. A cast-iron skillet is a good choice, however, if it isn't well seasoned, your eggs will stick like crazy, cleanup will be no fun and you'll be mad at me. For the vegetable mixture, I use a combination of zucchini, cremini mushrooms, red onions, red bell peppers and asparagus. Chop the veggies into chunks, toss with a bit of olive oil and grill in a grill basket until tender (stirring often). You can always chop the veggies smaller once they're grilled and cooled slightly. Measure 4 cups vegetables AFTER grilling.

SCAN FOR VIDEO!

YUM
Not a fan of feta?
Use old (sharp)
cheddar, Swiss or
goat's cheese instead.

YUMMER!
Sausage lovers: Layer
1 cup cooked and crumbled
Italian sausage over the
grilled veggies.

AN *eggsellent* CHOICE FOR BRUNCH

Nutritional
❧ INFO ❧

SNACKETIZERS
Turn Hummus Into Yummus!
(pages 26-27)

pumpkincredible
Per serving (2 tbsp): 64 calories, 4.4 g total fat (0.9 g saturated fat), 1.8 g protein, 4.3 g carbohydrate (1 g fiber, 0.8 g sugars), 0 mg cholesterol, 98 mg sodium

lemon-dillicious
Per serving (2 tbsp): 70 calories, 5 g total fat (1 g saturated fat), 2 g protein, 4 g carbohydrate (1 g fiber, 0 g sugars), 0 mg cholesterol, 130 mg sodium

sun-dried tomatOH!
Per serving (2 tbsp): 77 calories, 5.6 g total fat (1.1 g saturated fat), 2.1 g protein, 4.2 g carbohydrate (1 g fiber, 0.2 g sugars), 0 mg cholesterol, 141 mg sodium

guacHUMole
Per serving (2 tbsp): 62 calories, 4.7 g total fat (0.9 g saturated fat), 1.5 g protein, 3.6 g carbohydrate (1.3 g fiber, 0 g sugars), 0 mg cholesterol, 88 mg sodium

just beet it!
Per serving (2 tbsp): 56 calories, 3.8 g total fat (0.8 g saturated fat), 1.7 g protein, 3.8 g carbohydrate (1 g fiber, 0.6 g sugars), 0 mg cholesterol, 104 mg sodium

MEATLESS & MARVELOUS
Pesto is the Besto!
(pages 116-117)

Roasted Tomato Pesto
Per serving (1 tbsp): 67 calories, 6 g total fat (1 g saturated fat), 1.9 g protein, 2.3 g carbohydrate (0.7 g fiber, 1.2 g sugars), 3 mg cholesterol, 100 mg sodium

Classic Basil Pesto
Per serving (1 tbsp): 53 calories, 4.6 g total fat (0.9 g saturated fat), 1.5 g protein, 2.3 g carbohydrate (0.7 g fiber, 1.3 g sugars), 2 mg cholesterol, 76 mg sodium

Avocado & Spinach Pesto
Per serving (1 tbsp): 63 calories, 5.8 g total fat (0.8 g saturated fat), 1.5 g protein, 2.3 g carbohydrate (1.2 g fiber, 0.3 g sugars), 0 mg cholesterol, 44 mg sodium

FOWL TERRITORY
Happily Marinated Chicken
(pages 162-163)

Coconut Tandoori
Per serving (2 drumsticks, without skin): 231 calories, 11.2 g total fat (6.3 g saturated fat), 26 g protein, 4 g carbohydrate (1 g fiber, 1.2 g sugars), 82 mg cholesterol, 282 mg sodium

Honey Garlic & Ginger
Per serving (2 thighs, without skin): 295 calories, 11.5 g total fat (3.2 g saturated fat), 28 g protein, 20 g carbohydrate (0.4 g fiber, 16 g sugars), 98 mg cholesterol, 508 mg sodium

Maple, Balsamic & Rosemary
Per serving (1 breast, without skin): 269 calories, 7.8 g total fat (2.1 g saturated fat), 36 g protein, 12 g carbohydrate (0.2 g fiber, 11 g sugars), 96 mg cholesterol, 375 mg sodium

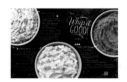

SIDE WAYS
Whip it Good!
(pages 214-215)

Roasted Garlic Cauliflower Mash
Per serving (about ½ cup): 140 calories, 8.7 g total fat (2.5 g saturated fat), 6 g protein, 12.5 g carbohydrate (4.5 g fiber, 5 g sugars), 12 mg cholesterol, 284 mg sodium

Squashed Potatoes
Per serving (about ½ cup): 152 calories, 3 g total fat (1.8 g saturated fat) 4.5 g protein, 28 g carbohydrate (2.2 g fiber, 3.4 g sugars), 10 mg cholesterol, 280 mg sodium

Maple-Butter Sweet Potatoes
Per serving (about ½ cup): 245 calories, 3.8 g total fat (2.7 g saturated fat), 3.6 g protein, 50 g carbohydrate (6.8 g fiber, 13 g sugars), 10 mg cholesterol, 302 mg sodium

Metric
CONVERSIONS

COMMON KITCHEN MEASUREMENTS

1 pint
2 cups
16 ounces
480 milliliters

1 quart
2 pints
4 cups
32 ounces
950 milliliters

1 gallon
4 quarts
8 pints
16 cups
128 ounces
3.8 liters

1 teaspoon
5 milliliters

1 tablespoon
3 teaspoons
15 milliliters

¼ cup
4 tablespoons
12 teaspoons
2 ounces
60 milliliters

1 cup
8 ounces
250 milliliters

TEMPERATURE CONVERSIONS
Fahrenheit to Celsius (°F to °C)

500 °F = 260 °C	350 °F = 180 °C
475 °F = 245 °C	325 °F = 160 °C
450 °F = 235 °C	300 °F = 150 °C
425 °F = 220 °C	275 °F = 135 °C
400 °F = 205 °C	250 °F = 120 °C
375 °F = 190 °C	225 °F = 110 °C

Index

Forever
GRATEFUL

YUM & YUMMER wouldn't be possible without their support, their creativity and their encouragement.

Janet Podleski

You would not be holding this book if it wasn't for my sister. Without our 20-year cookbook partnership and Janet's wealth of nutrition knowledge, corny sense of humor, contagious enthusiasm, dedication to helping others and perseverance when times were tough, I'd probably be sorting sugar snap peas at a vegetable processing plant waiting for quittin' time. Okay, perhaps I'm exaggerating about the peas, but not "The Pod." J-Pod, that is. Seriously, without Janet, my amazing cookbook career would never have happened.

Dave Chilton

I'm so lucky to have publishing guru and all-around great guy Dave Chilton (a.k.a. The Wealthy Barber) as my best friend. I get to pick his (genius) brain anytime I want on any subject I want, since he honestly knows something about everything! It's kinda freakish, actually. He's had a tremendously positive influence on my life and I'm so thankful for his advice and wisdom. Well, except the time he convinced me that cheering for the Detroit Lions was a good idea.

Leanne Cusack

I've known Leanne since 1996 when she interviewed Janet and me for CTV Ottawa in our very first television appearance. I've loved her ever since. The best advice Leanne gave me? "Just be yourself and SHINE!" I admire her for so many reasons, but mostly because she eats five bananas a day and never gains weight.

Fina Scroppo

My editor extraordinaire, fellow cookbook author and detail fanatic, Fina finessed her way through pages and pages of text like a true pro. Because she is a pro. Which is why I hired her. ☺ Also cuz she totally gets my slanguage.

Maureen Ross

Maureen is my personal cheerleader. When I bit off more than I could chew, "Mo" told me I was the world's best chewer—the greatest chewer ever—and to just keep chewing and doing what I was doing! She reassured me when I doubted myself, settled me down when stress got the best of me and even scrubbed my entire kitchen when I felt run down and flu-like. (Truth: I faked the whole flu thingy because I hate cleaning my kitchen. Sorry, Mo.)

REES + STAGER

I can thank Twitter for hooking me up with rock star foodie and social media maven Brittany Stager and the entire creative team at REES + STAGER: David, Gillian, Tanya, Catherine, Ben, Daniella, Stacey, Justin and Nikki. You helped turn my cookbook vision into reality and handled my annoying perfectionism with professionalism!

Chloe Jung

Everyone needs that one person they can bounce ideas off and get the honest-to-goodness truth in return. Chloe's that person. If something sucks, Chloe's gonna tell ya! If it's fantastic, she'll sing your praises from the highest mountain. She's brilliant, wise beyond her years and beautiful, too.

The Longarini Family

I'm fortunate to have great neighbors who also happen to love food, especially when "Meals on Heels" (that would be me!) arrived on their doorstep with recipe-testing samples. John Sr., John Jr., Leslie, Cassie and even dog Bentley were so supportive during the recipe development process, providing excellent *feed*back and loads of encouragement.

Pete McMenemy

I recently gave Pete three giant freezer baggies jam-packed with hundreds of loose grocery receipts and asked if he could sort them and add 'em up. He did. Quickly. Without complaining. That's the kind of guy you want handling your business accounting—for 20 years! (Pete: Remind me again why anti-frizz hairspray doesn't count as a recipe development expense?)

King Rico

My wild and crazy pooch, affectionately nicknamed "King Rico" since he truly rules the roost, has brought tremendous joy to my life ever since our eyes met in July 2011 at the Kitchener-Waterloo Humane Society. I love his zany personality, unstoppable energy and the fact that every morning upon waking he attempts a headstand. Yes, for real. (Or maybe it's a downward dog?)

If you enjoy YUM & YUMMER,
please tell your friends.
Thank you.

BW
Aug/28

MAPLE
SYRUP